CHRISTIAN CELEBRATIONS FOR SPRING AND SUMMER AGES 7-12

by Mary McMillan

illustrated by Janet Skiles

Cover by Janet Skiles

Shining Star Publications, Copyright © 1990

A Division of Good Apple, Inc.

ISBN No. 086653-530-6

Printing No. 987654321

Shining Star Publications
A Division of Good Apple, Inc.
1204 Buchanan, Box 299
Carthage, IL 62321-0299

The purchase of this book entitles the buyer to reproduce student activity pages for classroom use only. Any other use requires written permission from Shining Star Publications.

All rights reserved. Printed in the United States of America.

Unless otherwise indicated, the King James Version of the Bible was used in preparing the activities in this book.

TABLE OF CONTENTS

First Day of Spring
    Invitation 4
    Spring Cleaning Work Schedule 5
    Spring Cleaning Volunteer Badges 6
    Take Home Envelope 7
    Homemade Cinnamon Rolls 8

An Easter Celebration
    Invitation 9
    Decorations 10-11
    The Good News 12-14
    A Seder Meal 15

Arbor Day Celebration
    Invitation 16
    How to Plant a Tree 17
    Arbor Day Refreshments 18

Mother's Day
    Letters of Love 19-21
    Mother's Day Award 22
    Mother's Day Gift 23
    Breakfast in Bed 24

Memorial Day Celebration
    Invitation and Envelope 25-26
    Decorations 27-29
    Memorial Candle Holder 30
    Program 31

Father's Day
    Letters of Love 32-34
    Father's Day Award 35
    Father's Day Gift 36
    Avocado Omelet 37

Summer Celebration Camp-out
    Invitation and Checklist 38
    Camp-out Food 39
    Map It Out to the Campsite 40
    Sign-Up Duty Sheet 41
    Camp-out Fun 42

Independence Day Celebration
    Invitation 43
    A Door Poster Decoration 44
    A Bulletin Board Decoration and Patterns 45-48
    Independence Day Speeches 49
    Bumper Stickers 50
    Angel Food Delight 51

A Circus Celebration
    Invitation 52
    Circus Costumes 53-57

Shining Star Publications, Copyright © 1990, A division of Good Apple, Inc.   SS1820

Circus Memory Picture Frame 58
Pop-the-Balloon Booth 59-60
Circus Ice-Cream Cones 61

Celebrate Hawaii
   Invitation 62
   Decorations for Hawaiian Luau 63-66
   Luau Favor—Lei 67
   Place Mat for Luau 68
   Toothpick Straw Decorations 69
   The Lord's Prayer 69
   Hawaiian Words Puzzle 70
   Hawaiian Luau Feast 71

Celebrate the American Red Cross
   Invitation 72
   Decorations 73
   Red Cross Volunteer Checklist 74
   Red Cross Donation Envelope 75
   "Sack Supper" for the Homeless 76

First Day of School Celebration
   Door Poster—Listen to the Music 77-78
   Bulletin Board—Play the Notes that Count 79-80
   Door Poster—Shoot for the Stars 81
   Bulletin Board—Tour the Galaxy 82-84
   First Day of School Celebration Snacks 85-86

Grandparents' Day
   A Memory Gift Book 87-96

FIRST DAY OF SPRING
SPRING CLEANING CELEBRATION

(First day of Spring—March 20 or 21—Check current calendar.)
Spruce up the church grounds by having a spring cleaning celebration!

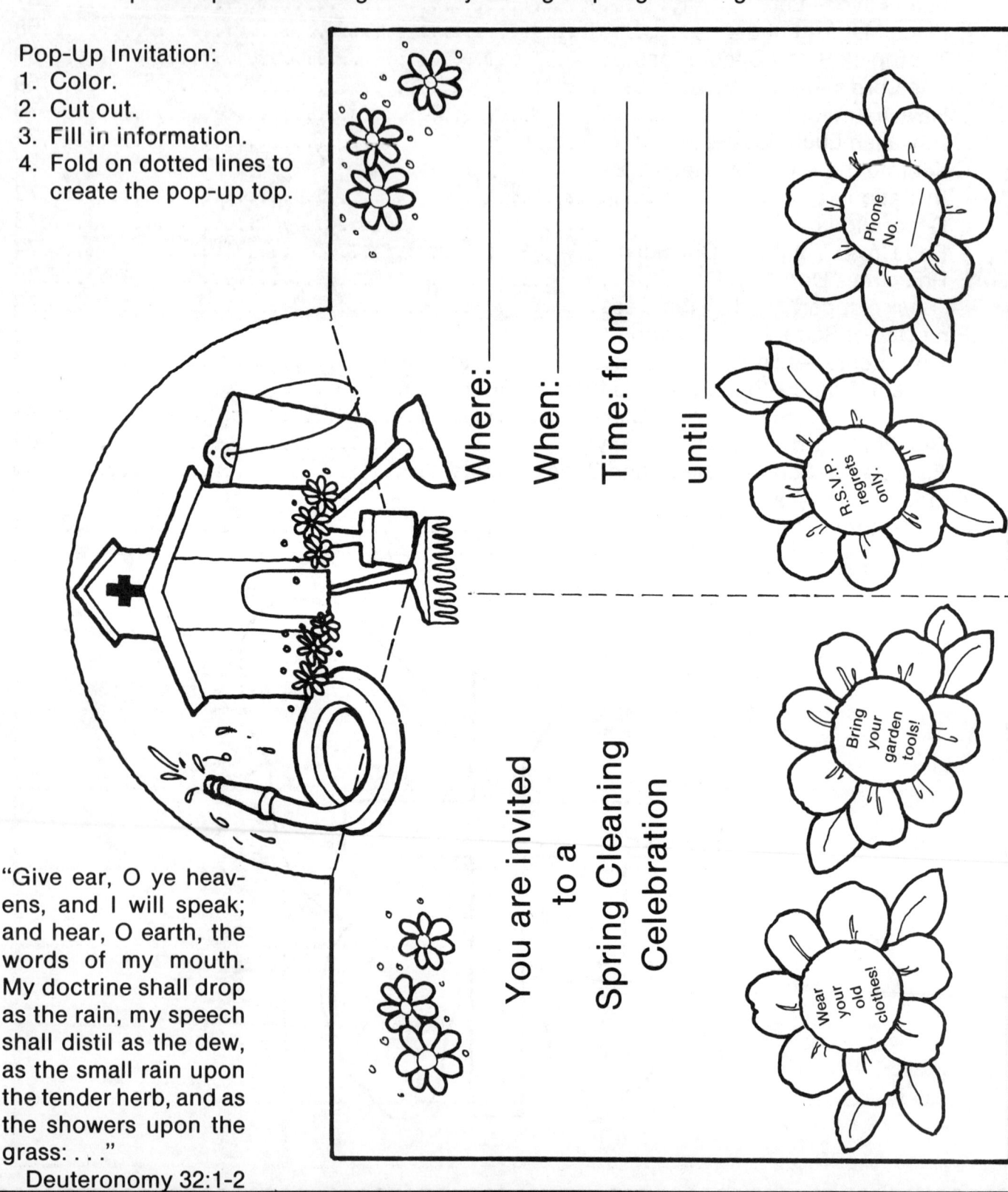

Pop-Up Invitation:
1. Color.
2. Cut out.
3. Fill in information.
4. Fold on dotted lines to create the pop-up top.

Where: _____
When: _____
Time: from _____
until _____

Phone No.

R.S.V.P. regrets only.

Bring your garden tools!

Wear your old clothes!

You are invited to a Spring Cleaning Celebration

"Give ear, O ye heavens, and I will speak; and hear, O earth, the words of my mouth. My doctrine shall drop as the rain, my speech shall distil as the dew, as the small rain upon the tender herb, and as the showers upon the grass: . . ."
Deuteronomy 32:1-2

SPRING CLEANING WORK SCHEDULE

Use the following work schedule sheet for volunteers to sign up for their spring cleaning assignments:

"And they went forth, and preached every where, the Lord working with them, . . . " Mark 16:20

SPRING CLEANING CELEBRATION SIGN UP WORK SCHEDULE

Work Assignment	Volunteer's Name	Time Volunteered
clean out flower beds		
trim the shrubs		
clean up rubbage		
rake up leftover leaves		
plant new flowers		
mow the grass		
bag up the grass cuttings		
sweep and wash the sidewalks		
clean the windows		
paint		

SPRING CLEANING VOLUNTEER BADGES

1. Color with bright markers. 2. Cut out. 3. Hand out to volunteers. 4. Instruct volunteers to wear badges in church on the Sunday morning after spring cleaning in order to recognize each one for the time they gave to the church.

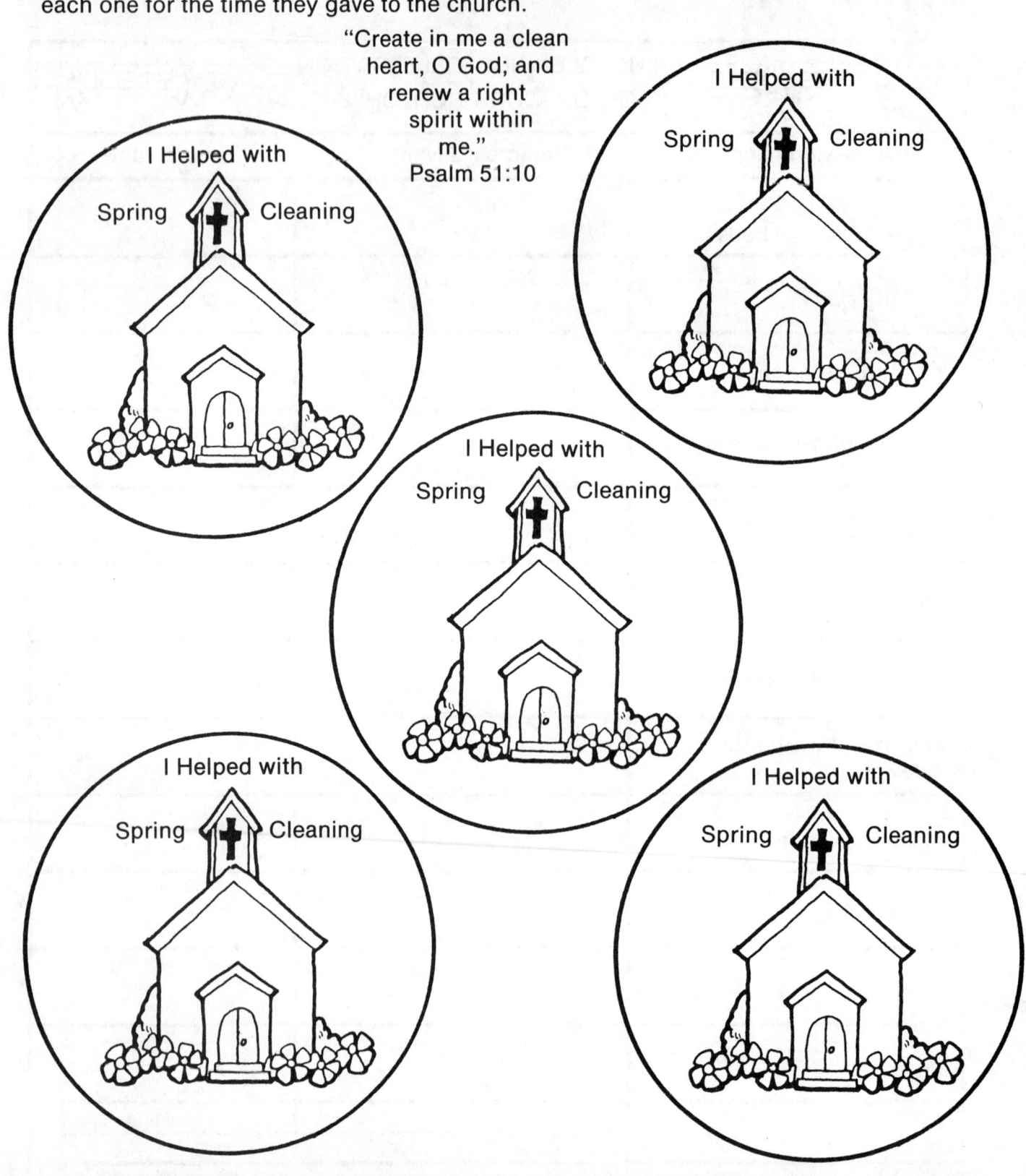

"Create in me a clean heart, O God; and renew a right spirit within me."
Psalm 51:10

I Helped with Spring Cleaning

I Helped with Spring Cleaning

I Helped with Spring Cleaning

I Helped with Spring Cleaning

I Helped with Spring Cleaning

TAKE HOME ENVELOPE

Take home an envelope of soil from the church garden. Give the envelope to a friend to spread God's word.

Envelope:
1. Color.
2. Cut out.
3. Fold down on dotted lines.
4. Glue areas along back and across bottom.

5. Fill with a handful of soil from the church garden.
6. Seal across top.
7. Share with a friend to spread God's word.

Enclosed in this envelope you will find soil from my church. Spread it in your garden and watch your plants grow!

"Then shall the earth yield her increase; and God, even our own God, shall bless us." Psalm 67:6

Given to: _____
Given by: _____

Shining Star Publications, Copyright © 1990, A division of Good Apple, Inc.

SS1820

Spring cleaning requires an early start, so start off the day with fresh fruit, orange juice, and homemade cinnamon rolls.

HOMEMADE CINNAMON ROLLS

Soften: 1 package active dry yeast in warm water

Combine: 1 cup scalded milk
¼ cup sugar
¼ cup shortening

Cool to lukewarm.

Add: 1½ cups flour

Beat in: softened yeast
1 egg

Gradually add: 2 more cups of flour

Form a soft dough and place in a greased bowl.

Cover and let rise (double its size).
(1½ to 2 hours)

Next: Cut dough in half. Roll out one half of the recipe at a time onto a floured surface. (Roll each half into a large rectangular shape.)

Combine: ½ cup sugar
3 tablespoons melted butter
2 teaspoons cinnamon

Spread: one half of mixture over each rectangle

Roll each rectangle lengthwise.

Seal the edges and cut into 1-inch slices.

Place on greased pan. Cover and let rise 30 to 40 minutes.

Bake: 375 degrees for 20 to 25 minutes.

Let cool and frost.

Frosting: Combine 2 to 3 tablespoons of milk with 2 cups of confectioners' sugar and 1 teaspoon vanilla. Spread over cooled cinnamon rolls.

AN EASTER CELEBRATION

(Palm Sunday is the last Sunday before Easter and the beginning of Holy Week. Easter usually falls on the first Sunday after the first full moon on or after March 21. Check your current calendar.)

Invitation: 1. Color. 2. Cut out. 3. Fill in information. 4. Hand out and instruct guests to fill in Bible scriptures as well as bring completed invitation to the celebration to share Christ's teachings with friends.

You are invited to an Easter celebration of Christ's teachings!

Where: _____
When: _____
Time: from _____ until _____

Your special instructions are to use your Bible to fill in the blanks with Christ's teachings.

Mark 16:15

Mark 12:30

". . . If thou canst believe, all things are possible to him that believeth."   Mark 9:23

Luke 23:43

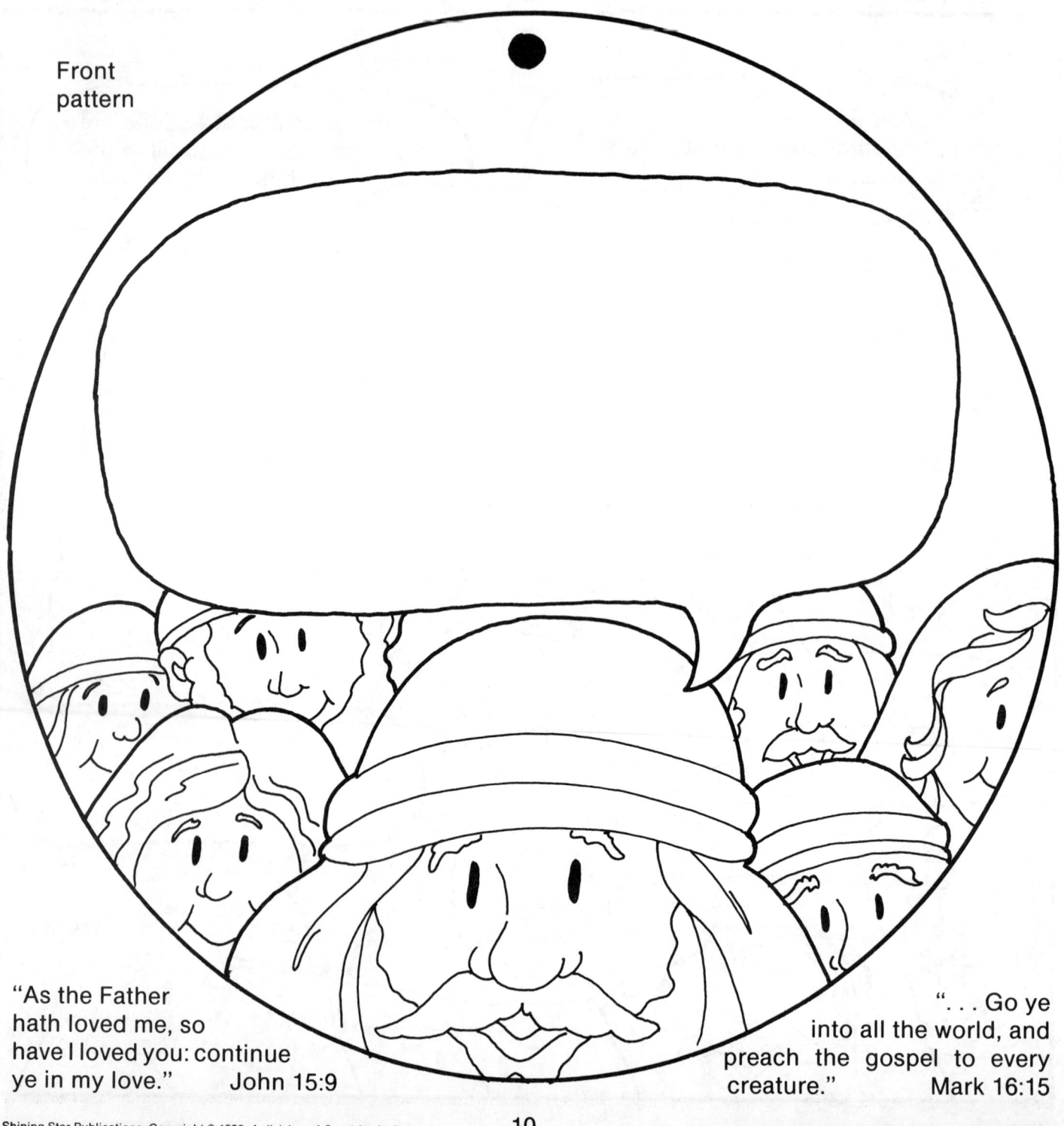

DECORATIONS

Decoration:
1. Enlarge front and back patterns provided. 2. Color with bright-colored markers. 3. Cut out. 4. Glue front to back. 5. Use the New Testament Bible to locate Christ's teachings leading up to the resurrection. Fill in one Bible verse on each side of decoration. 6. Punch hole at top and hang from ceiling.

"And thou shalt love the Lord thy God with all thy heart, and with all thy soul, and with all thy mind, and with all thy strength: . . ." Mark 12:30

". . . blessed are they that have not seen, and yet have believed." John 20:29

Front pattern

"As the Father hath loved me, so have I loved you: continue ye in my love." John 15:9

". . . Go ye into all the world, and preach the gospel to every creature." Mark 16:15

Shining Star Publications, Copyright © 1990, A division of Good Apple, Inc.

10

SS1820

DECORATIONS

Decorations:

"... and, lo, I am with you always, even unto the end of the world. Amen."
Matthew 28:20

"... My house shall be called the house of prayer; ..."   Matthew 21:13

Back pattern

"... Follow me."
John 21:19

"... Thou shalt love thy neighbour as thyself."
Matthew 22:39

"... Suffer little children, and forbid them not, to come unto me: for of such is the kingdom of heaven."   Matthew 19:14

SHARE THE CELEBRATION WITH THE GOOD NEWS

Have your guests participate by completing each page of the newspaper that follows. Then, spread THE GOOD NEWS around by passing the newspaper out to friends, neighbors, church goers, etc.

THE GOOD NEWS

FREE   VOL. 1, NO.1

FEATURE STORY: SUGGESTIONS FOR SPREADING THE GOOD NEWS

Written by _____

"... Go ye into all the world, and preach the gospel to every creature."
Mark 16:15

I BELIEVE BECAUSE

Written by _____

"... blessed are they that have not seen, and yet have believed," John 20:29

WAYS IN WHICH I WILL FOLLOW

Written by _____

"... Follow me."
John 21:19

Shining Star Publications, Copyright © 1990, A division of Good Apple, Inc.

SS1820

PAGE 2—THE GOOD NEWS

LOVE THY NEIGHBOR LIST

Written by _____

1. _____
2. _____
3. _____
4. _____
5. _____
6. _____
7. _____
8. _____

". . . Thou shalt love thy neighbour as thyself."
Matthew 22:39

A SPECIAL EASTER PRAYER

Written by _____

WHAT COMMUNION MEANS TO ME

Written by _____

"And he took bread, . . and gave unto them, saying, This is my body which is given for you: this do in remembrance of me."   Luke 22:19

PAGE 3—THE GOOD NEWS

GOD IS WITH ME ALWAYS

Written by _____

_____
_____
_____
_____
_____
_____

"... and, lo, I am with you always, even unto the end of the world. Amen."
Matthew 28:20

THE GOOD NEWS

Newspaper Staff:
The following Good News reporters "... love the Lord thy God with all thy heart, ..."   Mark 12:30

_____
_____
_____
_____
_____
_____
_____
_____
_____

THE LORD'S PRAYER

Copied from the Bible by: _____
_____

"... Our Father which art in heaven,

Hallowed be thy name. ..."

_____
_____
_____
_____
_____
_____
_____
_____
_____
_____

Luke 11:2-4

A SEDER MEAL

A seder meal is a Jewish ceremonial dinner held on the first evening of Passover. Jesus met with His disciples to eat the Passover meal.

". . . The Master saith, Where is the guestchamber, where I shall eat the passover with my disciples?" Mark 14:14

For your Easter celebration, prepare a seder meal similar to that which Jesus might have shared with His disciples.
Some suggestions might be roasted lamb with herbs and spices, homemade bread, fresh fruits such as figs and grapes, and a grape drink. Research other foods that might have been prepared.

HERBED LEG OF LAMB

Brown lamb in large skillet with one to two tablespoons of butter.

Add 1½ cups of water plus 1 teaspoon of salt.

Cover skillet. Cook 1 hour over low heat.

Melt 2 tablespoons butter. Mix in ¼ cup flour. Cook and stir until browned. Pour over meat. Cook and stir until thickened.

Then, add ½ cup water plus 1 garlic clove, minced; ⅛ teaspoon dried marjoram, crushed; and 1 tablespoon parsley. Also, sprinkle a small amount of ground mace.

Cover and cook until tender. (1 to 1½ hours)

GRAPE DRINK

Mix: 8 cups grape juice
   1½ cups orange juice
   1 cup sugar
   ⅓ cup lemon juice
   ⅓ cup lime juice

Chill 1 hour. Add 3 cups ginger ale.

Pour into punch bowl and float orange and lemon slices on top.

ARBOR DAY CELEBRATION

(In southern states and Hawaii—celebrated on various dates from December to March. In most northern states—celebrated in April or May. In California—celebrated on March 7. Check a local, current calendar.)

"The trees of the Lord are full of sap; . . ."

Psalm 104:16

Celebrate the Lord and Arbor Day by planting trees around your church yard!

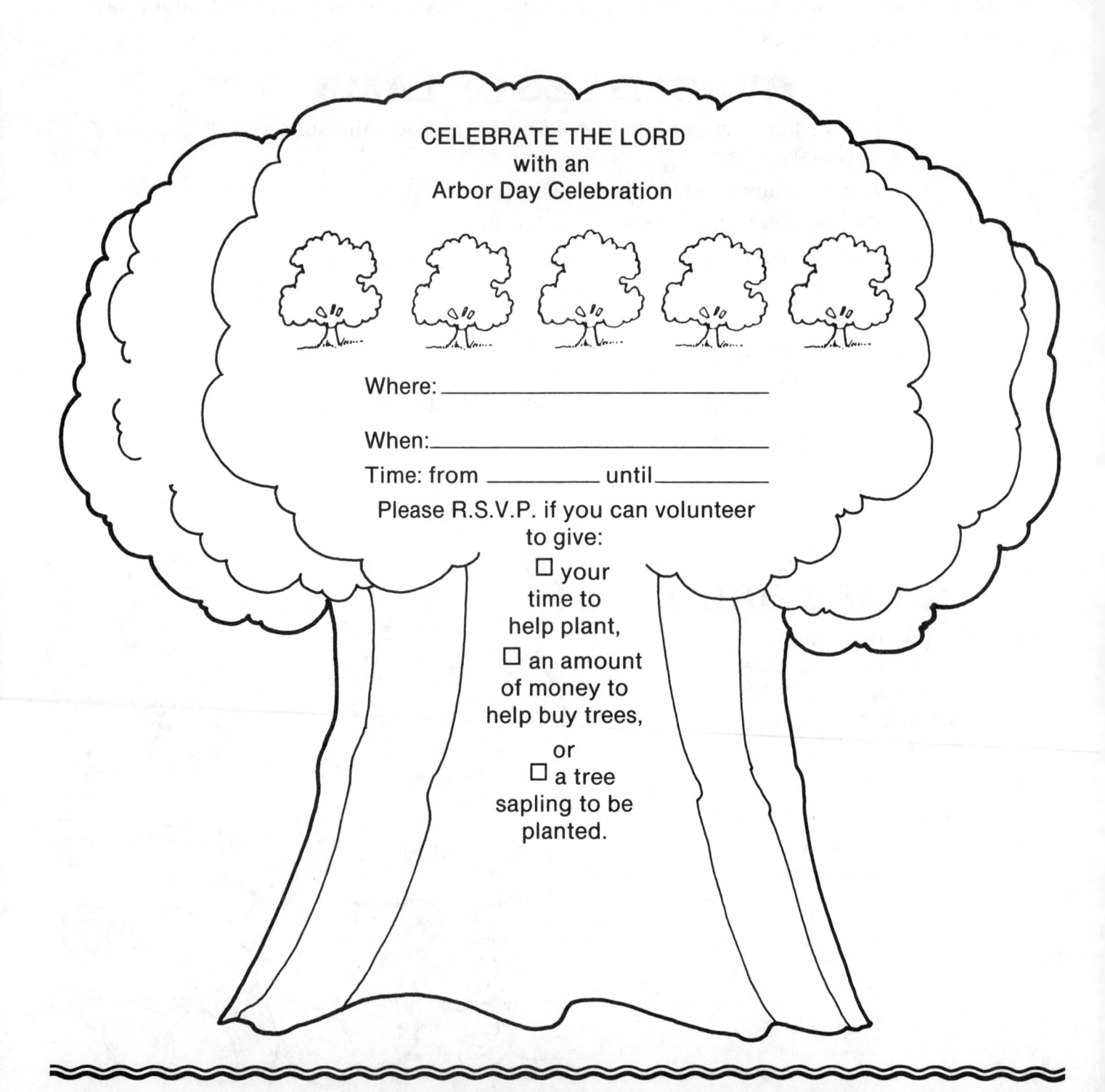

CELEBRATE THE LORD
with an
Arbor Day Celebration

Where: _____

When: _____

Time: from _____ until _____

Please R.S.V.P. if you can volunteer to give:

☐ your time to help plant,

☐ an amount of money to help buy trees,

or

☐ a tree sapling to be planted.

HOW TO PLANT A TREE

Run off one copy for every volunteer to take home as a reference for planting trees at home or elsewhere.

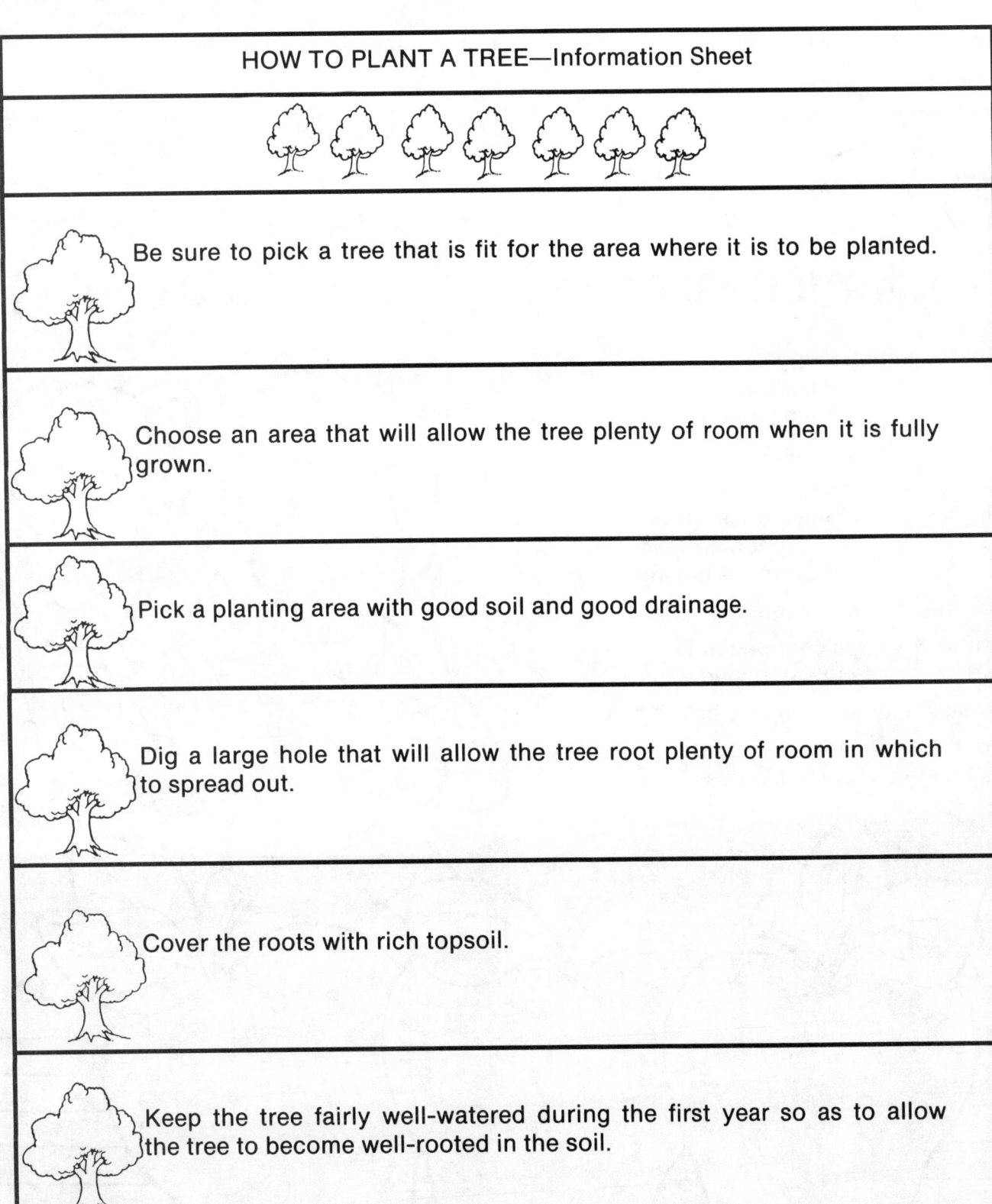

HOW TO PLANT A TREE—Information Sheet
Be sure to pick a tree that is fit for the area where it is to be planted.
Choose an area that will allow the tree plenty of room when it is fully grown.
Pick a planting area with good soil and good drainage.
Dig a large hole that will allow the tree root plenty of room in which to spread out.
Cover the roots with rich topsoil.
Keep the tree fairly well-watered during the first year so as to allow the tree to become well-rooted in the soil.

ARBOR DAY REFRESHMENTS

"Even so every good tree bringeth forth good fruit; . . ." Matthew 7:17

Celebrate the Lord's blessings—serve fruits from the trees!

walnuts

apricots   apples   pecans   oranges   cherries   bananas

peaches

chestnuts

APPLE NUT CAKE

Beat together: 2 eggs
              2 cups sugar
              1 teaspoon vanilla

Beat in: ½ cup cooking oil

Sift together: 2 cups flour
              2 teaspoons cinnamon
              1 teaspoon nutmeg
              2 teaspoons baking soda

Stir into egg and sugar mixture.

Stir in: 1½ cups chopped nuts
        3 to 4 cups chopped apples

Grease and flour a round bundt pan.

Pour mixture into prepared pan. Bake at 325 degrees for 60 minutes.

Shining Star Publications, Copyright © 1990, A division of Good Apple, Inc.

SS1820

MOTHER'S DAY LETTERS OF LOVE

(Mother's Day is the second Sunday in May.)

"As one whom his mother comforteth, so will I comfort you; and ye shall be comforted in Jerusalem."

Isaiah 66:13

Use your Mother's Day stationery provided to write your mother a "letter of love." Fold on the dotted lines. Cut out and glue the sticker provided to seal the letter. Give to Mom for Mother's Day!

Sticker seal

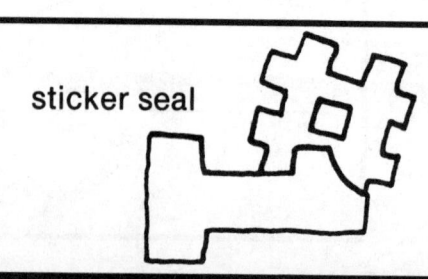

LETTERS OF LOVE

sticker seal

LETTERS OF LOVE
sticker seal

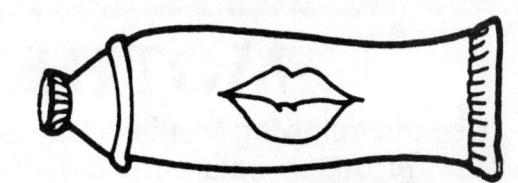

MOTHER'S DAY AWARD

Use the following Mother's Day award to celebrate your mother.
1. Run off on colored paper. 2. Glue to the center of a large doily leaving a ruffled border around the edges. 3. Fill in information and give to your Mother for a Mother's Day surprise.

Be sure to let your mother know just how much you really appreciate what she does for you!

"... and forsake not the law of thy mother:"
Proverbs 1:8

Mother's Day Award

My Mother

_____

is a Super #1 Mom because

_____

_____

_____

Border text: MOTHERS PLAY · MOTHERS LAUGH · MOTHERS CRY · MOTHERS WORRY · MOTHERS PRAY · MOTHERS TEACH · MOTHERS LOVE · MOTHERS HELP · MOTHERS HUG · MOTHERS CARE · MOTHERS SHARE

MOTHER'S DAY GIFT

Mothers are constantly doing things for their children through love. Use the Mother's Day Gift certificate below. Have your mother fill in ten things that you can do for her. Remember to show your mother how much you appreciate her for all she does for you.

Mother's Day Certificate:

1. Color.
2. Cut out.
3. Insert inside section by gluing to the inner side.
4. Fold on dotted lines and glue along dotted edge.
5. Give to Mom for Mother's Day.

Inside Section:

Happy Mother's Day
Make a list of ten things I can do for you

Mother's Day Gift
Given in love by

BREAKFAST IN BED

Help your mother celebrate Mother's Day by serving her a healthy, low calorie breakfast in bed.

LOW CALORIE FRENCH TOAST
(NO CHOLESTEROL)

Mix: ½ cup no cholesterol Egg Beaters

1-2 pkg. sugar substitute

1 teaspoon cinnamon

Dip into mixture: 2 slices of reduced calorie bread.

Place bread slices in hot skillet sprayed with PAM (a low fat, no stick cooking spray).

Brown bread slices on both sides.

Serve with 2 tablespoons of low calorie syrup.

When your mother has finished be sure to wash the dishes and clean the kitchen. Then offer to be your mother's partner for a two-mile walk.

"Then shall thy light break forth as the morning, and thine health shall spring forth speedily: and thy righteousness shall go before thee; the glory of the Lord shall be thy rearward." Isaiah 58:8

MEMORIAL DAY CELEBRATION

(Most states celebrate Memorial Day the last Monday in May. However, you should check your local state calendar for the date of this legal holiday.)

Memorial Day is a patriotic holiday set aside to honor Americans who gave their lives in war to help preserve the freedom of this country.

Plan a Memorial Day celebration. Have each boy and girl in your group invite a veteran to be his or her guest partner for the celebration. Enclose the ribbon pattern provided in each envelope. Request that each veteran write on the ribbon the name of a friend who lost his or her life while fighting for our country's freedom. Ask that the ribbon be brought to the celebration.

". . . I am the resurrection, and the life: . . ."
John 11:25

YOU ARE INVITED
TO BE
A GUEST OF HONOR
AT A
MEMORIAL DAY CELEBRATION

Where: _____
When: _____
Time: from _____
until _____
Your guest partner will be
_____
R.S.V.P. regrets only please
Phone number _____

In Memory Of

RIBBON INSTRUCTIONS:
1. Please fill in the name of a friend who lost his or her life while helping to preserve the freedom of America.
2. Please bring the ribbon with you to our Memorial Day Celebration. (Cut away at dotted line)

Invitation Envelope:

1. Fold bottom and sides together along dotted lines.
2. Slide in invitation from top.
3. Fold top side down along dotted line and glue.
4. Fill in name and pass out to your guest partner.

A MEMORIAL DAY CELEBRATION INVITATION FOR

"... he that believeth in me, though he were dead, yet shall he live:"

John 11:25

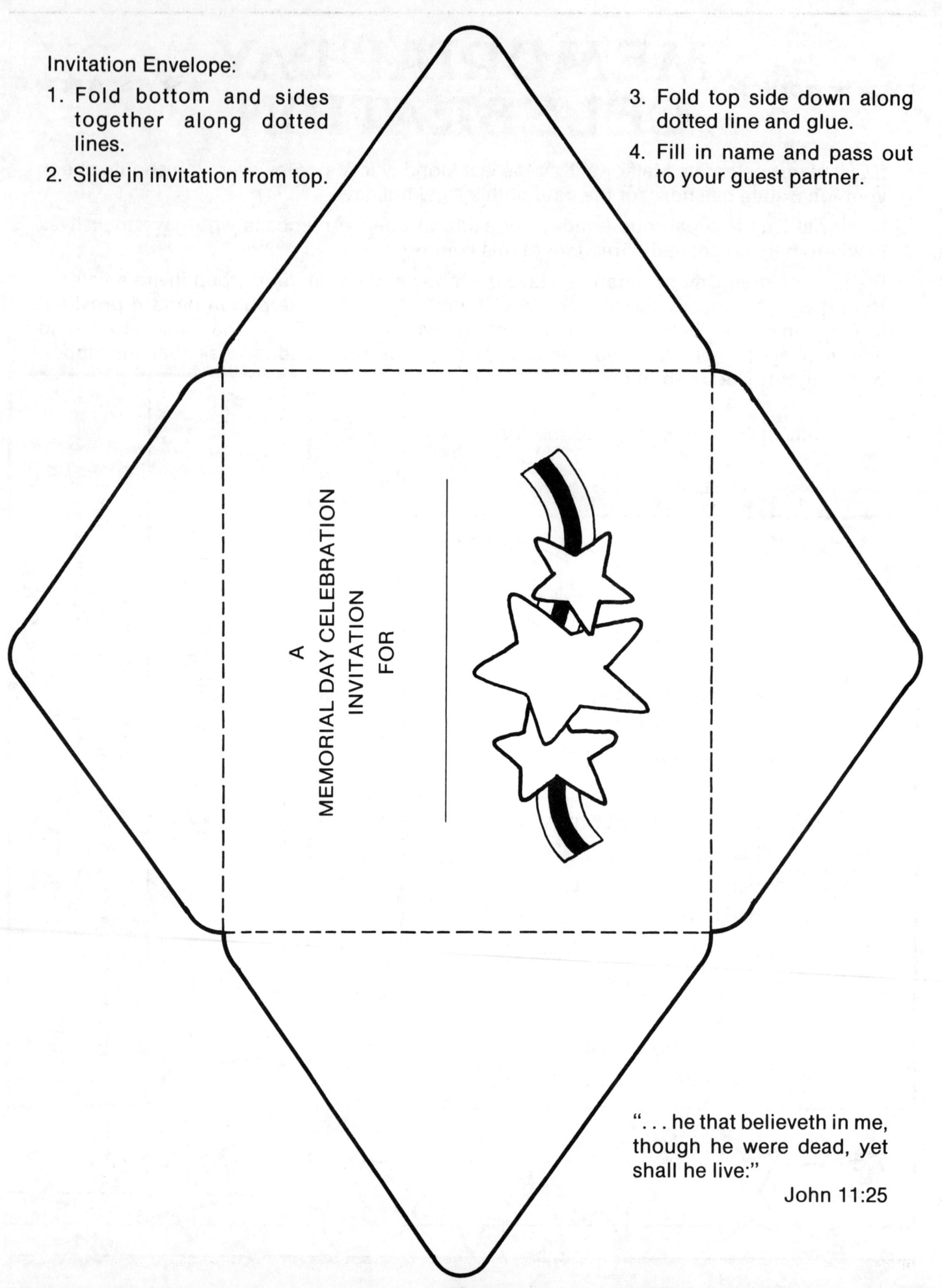

DECORATIONS
MEMORIAL TREE

1. Take a bare branch from a tree. Spray the branch with white spray paint. Let dry.

2. Make a stand for the branch with four blocks of wood—¾" × 1½" × 6". Nail the four blocks of wood around the base of the tree branch as shown in the diagram.

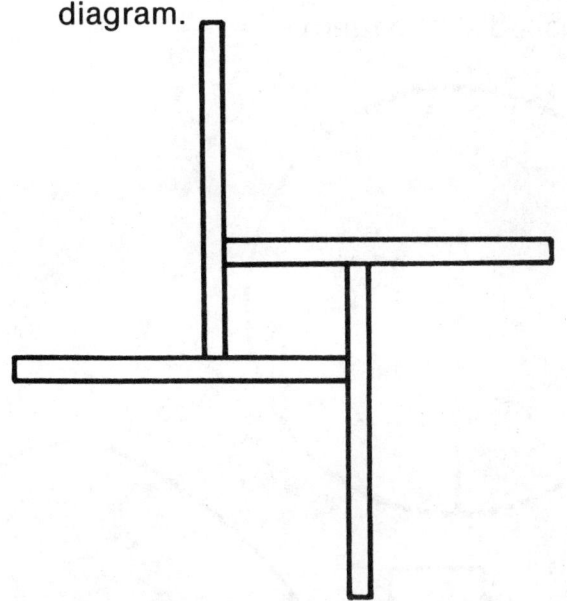

3. Stand the tree branch on the top of a table placed in the center of the room. (Before placing the tree branch, cover the table with a white tablecloth.)

4. Use the skirt pattern provided on the next page to make a cover for the base of the tree.

5. Use the cross patterns provided on page 29 to make white crosses. Hang the crosses from the branches of the tree with colored yarn.

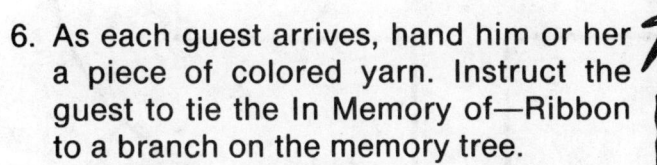

6. As each guest arrives, hand him or her a piece of colored yarn. Instruct the guest to tie the In Memory of—Ribbon to a branch on the memory tree.

"And whosoever liveth and believeth in me shall never die. . . ." John 11:26

SKIRT PATTERN FOR MEMORIAL TREE

1. Cut a circle from white material. (Circle diameter—24") Sew a ½" to 1" hem along the rough edges.

2. Use a pencil to trace the butterfly pattern provided around the bottom outer edge. Go over the penciled lines with colored Puff paint. (Puff paint can be purchased in almost any art supply store or art department.) Use a hot blow dryer to "puff" the paint or follow other directions on the Puff-paint container.

3. Cover the base of the memorial tree with the finished skirt pattern.

(Cut slit from outer edge to center of skirt circle to enable the skirt to be wrapped around base of tree.)

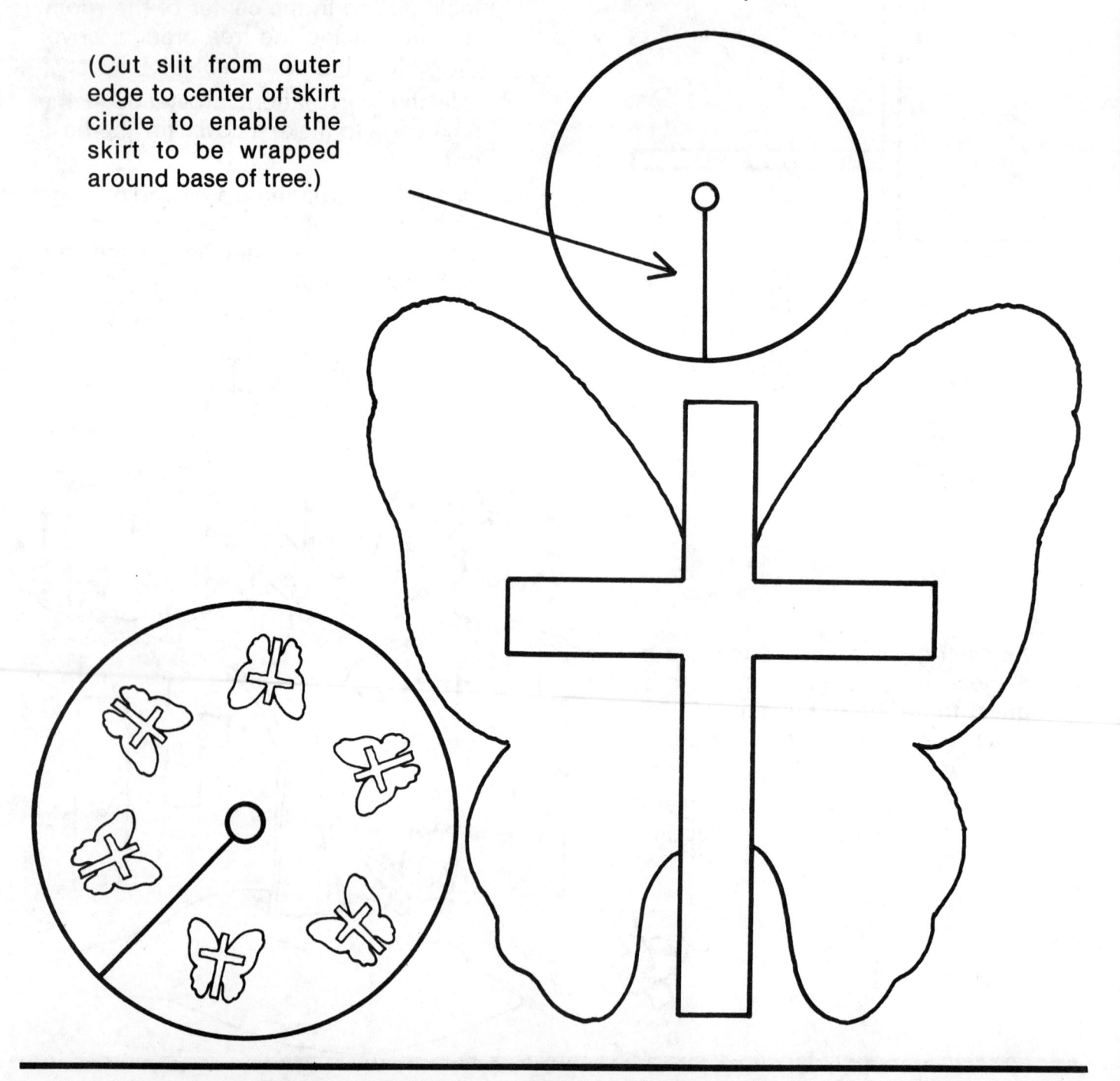

CROSS PATTERNS FOR MEMORIAL TREE

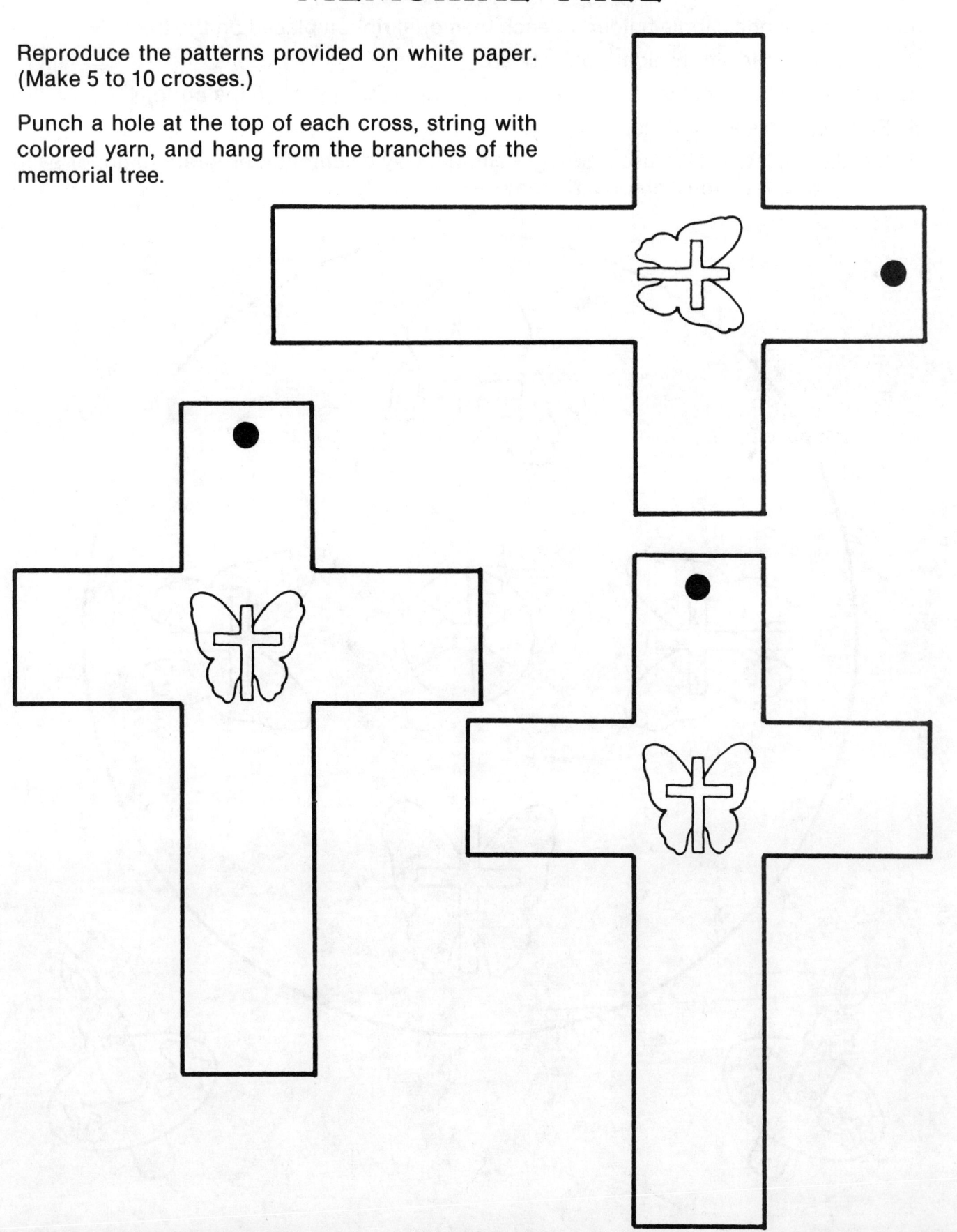

Reproduce the patterns provided on white paper. (Make 5 to 10 crosses.)

Punch a hole at the top of each cross, string with colored yarn, and hang from the branches of the memorial tree.

MEMORIAL CANDLE HOLDER

1. Reproduce one candle holder for each memorial ribbon placed on the tree.
2. Cut from white, lightweight poster board.
3. Cut along slits in center and push a white candle through from the bottom.
4. Place on table around memorial tree.
5. Candle holders will be used during Memorial Day celebration program to honor each name written on the memorial ribbons.

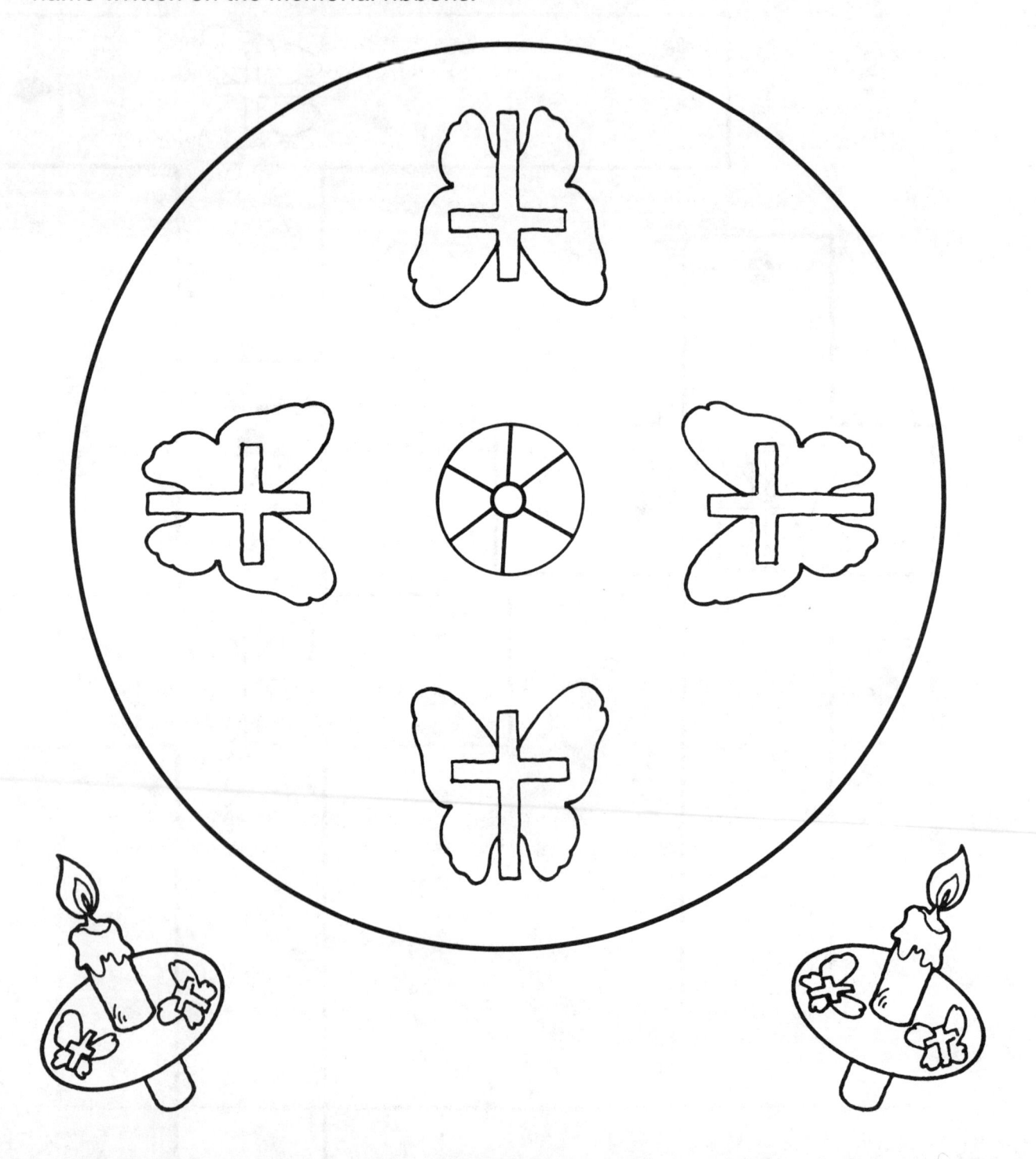

MEMORIAL DAY CELEBRATION PROGRAM

Duplicate one for each person attending the celebration. Set up memorial table as instructed on page 27. Place candles and candle holders on table around the tree. Follow celebration procedure as written on program.

PROGRAM

(When the program begins, have each group member and guest partner stand side by side in a circle around the Memorial table in the center of the room.)

Leader: ". . . I am the resurrection, and the life: he that believeth in me, though he were dead, yet shall he live: And whosoever liveth and believeth in me shall never die. . . ."

John 11:25-26

1st Group Member:
1. walks to the memorial table in the center of the room,
2. lights a candle from the lit candle the group leader is holding,
3. reads a name from one of the ribbons hanging from the memorial tree,
4. and repeats the following, "I light this candle in memory of _____.
(name)
5. returns to his original place in the circle,
6. and passes the candle holder over to his/her guest partner to hold until the end of the ceremony.

2nd Group Member: and the others repeat the pattern and so on until all the names from the memorial tree have been honored.

Leader: "For the Lord himself shall descend from heaven with a shout, with the voice of the archangel, and with the trump of God: and the dead in Christ shall rise first:"

I Thessalonians 4:16

All: "Then we which are alive and remain shall be caught up together with them in the clouds, to meet the Lord in the air: and so shall we ever be with the Lord."

I Thessalonians 4:17

FATHER'S DAY
LETTERS OF LOVE

(Father's Day is the third Sunday in June.)

"My son, hear the instruction of thy father, . . ."   Proverbs 1:8

Dads like to be told how much they are loved, too. Choose one of the following samples of stationery and write your father a "letter of love."

1. Color. 2. Cut out. 3. Write letter. 4. Fold on dotted lines. 5. Slide tab into slit to close.

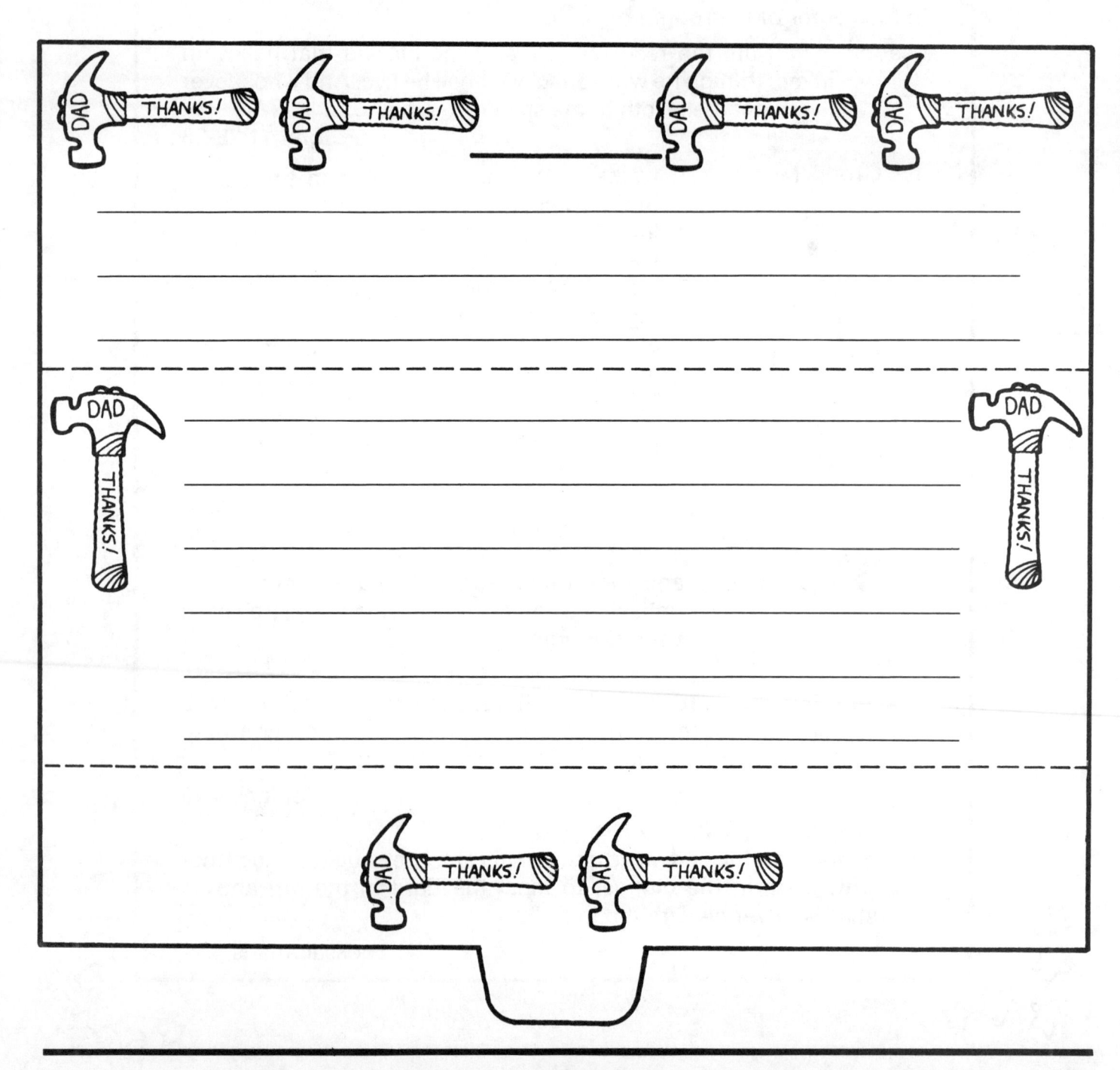

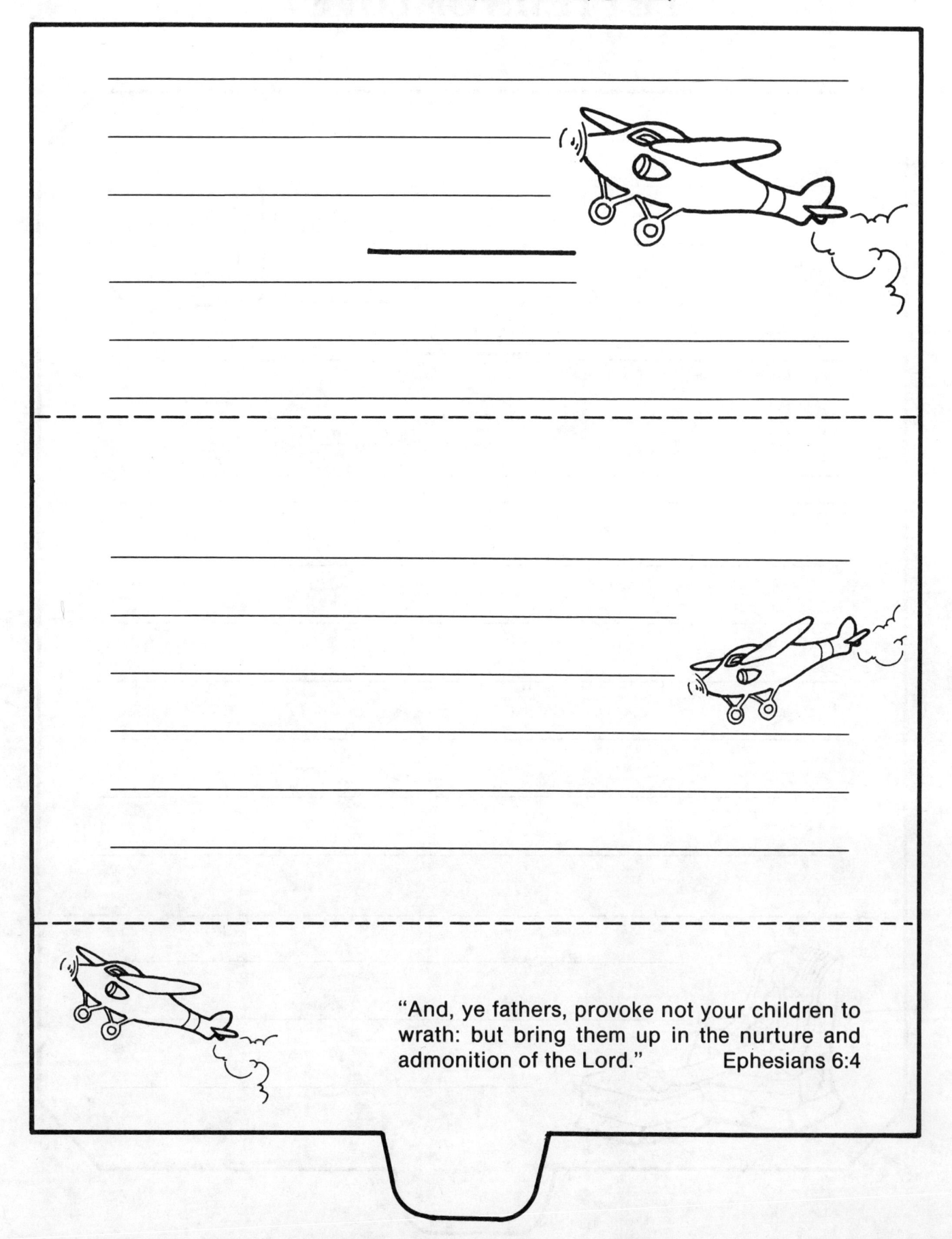

LETTERS OF LOVE

_____

_____

_____

          _____

_____

_____

_____

- -

_____

_____

_____

_____

_____

_____

- -

"And, ye fathers, provoke not your children to wrath: but bring them up in the nurture and admonition of the Lord." Ephesians 6:4

LETTERS OF LOVE

FATHER'S DAY AWARD

Use the following Father's Day award to celebrate your father. 1. Duplicate onto colored paper. 2. Glue to the center of a piece of black construction paper, leaving a black border around the award. 3. Fill in the information and present to Dad.

FATHERS PRAY . . . FATHERS WORRY . . . FATHERS LAUGH . . .

FATHER'S DAY AWARD

FATHERS PLAY . . . FATHERS CARE . . . FATHERS LOVE . . . FATHERS TEACH . . .

FATHERS DISCIPLINE . . . FATHERS TALK . . . FATHERS LISTEN . . .

My Dad

_____

is the best because

_____
_____
_____

FATHERS HUG . . . FATHERS PROTECT . . . FATHERS SHINE . . .

Shining Star Publications, Copyright © 1990, A division of Good Apple, Inc.   SS1820

FATHER'S DAY GIFT

Because fathers spend so much time working for their families, they don't always have as much time as they would like to have to spend with their children.

Give your father the gift of time. Allow him to choose what the two of you will do with that precious gift.

"My times are in thy hand: . . ." Psalm 31:15

HAPPY FATHER'S DAY

My gift to you is time.

Fill in six ways in which you would like for me to spend time with you.

_____   _____

_____   _____

_____   _____

Treat your dad to a special Father's Day breakfast. Serve him an avocado omelet and a bowl of fresh fruit.

AVOCADO OMELET

Melt: 2 tablespoons of non-cholesterol type margarine in a small skillet.

Pour in: 4 eggs and cook three to four minutes over a slow heat. Use spatula to make sure the raw eggs cook evenly. Then remove from heat. Egg Beaters may be substituted for eggs.

Sprinkle with: ½ to ¾ cup grated Monterey Jack cheese.

Place in: 325 degree oven until cheese melts.

In the meantime, mix: ½ avocado
⅛ cup sour cream
1 tablespoon chopped green chilies
2 teaspoons chopped green onion
pinch of salt

Pour: avocado mixture over melted cheese.

Fold over omelet and place in oven for 3 to 5 more minutes.

Serve to your dad along with a bowl of fresh melon, bananas, pineapple, apples, raisins, etc.

After breakfast invite your father to play a game of tennis, ride bicycles, or go fishing. Let him choose. After all, it is Father's Day!

SUMMER CELEBRATION CAMP-OUT

(First day of summer—June 20 or 21—check your calendar.)

"God is faithful, by whom ye were called unto the fellowship of his Son Jesus Christ our Lord."   I Corinthians 1:9

Invitations: 1. Color. 2. Cut out. 3. Fill in information including what foods you would like each guest to bring. (See suggestions for camp-out food on following page.)

SUMMER CELEBRATION CAMP-OUT

Celebrate with: _____

Where: _____
(map provided)

When: _____

Time: from _____ until _____

Please R.S.V.P. Phone # _____

Checklist:
- a cot or sleeping bag ☐
- pillow and blankets ☐
- bath towel and bar of soap ☐
- toothbrush and toothpaste ☐
- non-breakable plate and cup ☐
- knife, fork, and spoon ☐
- an extra pair of dry shoes ☐
- warm jacket, sweatshirts, jeans ☐
- insect spray ☐
- first-aid cream and bandages ☐
- flashlight and extra batteries ☐
- extra clothes, including socks and underwear ☐
- toilet paper ☐
- comb and brush ☐
- other _____

Parents willing to chaperone? yes ☐ no ☐
Please call # _____
Tent? How many? _____
Foods? _____
Other? _____

Shining Star Publications, Copyright © 1990, A division of Good Apple, Inc.   SS1820

CAMP-OUT FOOD

Make a trail snack mix for each camper by mixing together 1 cup of chocolate chips, peanuts, raisins, dried banana chips, coconut, and dried cereals.

Make instant hot cocoa by mixing with hot water over the campfire.

Roast marshmallows over the campfire. Serve over a piece of chocolate on a graham cracker.

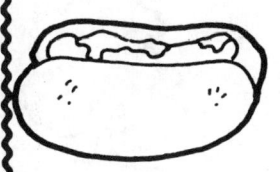

Roast frankfurters over campfire. Serve on hot dog bun with chili and mustard or catsup.

Have on hand plenty of fresh and dried fruits for munching.

Baked potatoes wrapped in foil under coals.

Wrap buttered corn-on-the-cob with foil and place under hot coals to cook.

Put 1 tablespoon vegetable oil and ⅛ to ¼ cup popcorn in a loosely covered aluminum foil piece. Place over hot coals until popcorn has stopped popping.

Cook a stew in a tin can (empty coffee can will do) by mixing a can of soup, a small onion, sliced carrots, sliced potatoes, sliced celery, and very lean hamburger meat. Cook slowly over coals until meat is thoroughly cooked. Salt and pepper to taste.

Camping equipment might include: a first-aid kit, a can opener, large plastic trash bags, pots and pans for cooking and cleaning, a sewing kit, a compass, fresh drinking water and drinking cups, napkins, paper towels, extra flashlights, a hammer, a saw, an axe, and just in case of rain—plastic ground covers for tents, raincoats, rubber boots, and plenty of plastic bags in which to store food, clothes, etc.

MAP IT OUT TO THE CAMPSITE

Provide a map for each guest. Use the symbols shown in the map legend to draw a map to your campsite. Be sure to include a telephone number if possible just in case someone gets lost along the way.

Start here

Phone # _____

Campsite
House
Building
Parking Lot
Railroad
School
Church
Lake
River
Trees
Road
Fence
Trail

"And God said, Let the earth bring forth grass, the herb yielding seed, and the fruit tree yielding fruit . . . and it was so." Genesis 1:11

N W←→E S

SIGN-UP DUTY SHEET

Use the sign-up duty sheet to "assign" camp-out duties to your guests. Be sure that everyone shares in the fun and work as well.

CAMP-OUT SIGN-UP DUTY SHEET

Cooking: (Adult supervision)
_____
_____
_____

Hauling Water:
_____
_____
_____

Cleanup Crew:
_____
_____
_____

Set Up Tents:
_____
_____
_____
_____

Pick Up Trash:
_____
_____
_____

Campfire Storytellers:
_____
_____
_____
_____

Building Fire: (Adult supervision)
_____
_____
_____

Setting Table:
_____
_____
_____

Dishwashers:
_____
_____
_____

In Charge of Fishing Equipment:
_____
_____
_____

Hanging Clothesline for Wet Clothes:
_____
_____

Song Leaders:
_____
_____

In Charge of Games:
_____
_____

Other:
_____
_____

". . . Fear God, and keep his commandments: for this is the whole duty of man."
Ecclesiastes 12:13

CAMP-OUT FUN

"The glory of the Lord shall endure for ever: the Lord shall rejoice in his works."
Psalm 104:31

CAMP-OUT SCAVENGER HUNT

Divide the campers into teams. Give each team a list of things to find within or nearby the campsite within a set period of time. (Be sure to assign an adult to each team if it becomes necessary to wander too far away from the campsite.)

The winning team is the one that returns with the greatest number of objects from the list within the set amount of time. Suggestions for a camp-out scavenger hunt list might be:

- a bird's feather
- a red leaf
- a piece of moss
- a flint rock
- a chalk rock
- a fossil
- a nut
- a seed
- a reed or foxtail
- a lily pad
- a piece of spider web
- a turkey tail feather
- a mushroom
- a discarded piece of a bird's eggshell (DO NOT disturb an egg or nest that is in use.)
- a weed
- a fallen dead branch
- a clover leaf
- a picture (drawn or taken with camera) of an animal or bird actually seen on the hunt

(Please stress the importance of not disturbing nature. Scavengers should seek out objects that are no longer being used by nature itself—dead and broken branches, feathers fallen to the ground, etc. Or, another suggestion might be to provide each team with markers and paper on which to draw maps or pictures of each object they find so as not to disturb anything nature has provided.)

Other camping ideas:

PLAY BASEBALL

PLAY VOLLEYBALL

MAKE A TREE SWING

TENT CONTEST—WHICH TEAM CAN PUT THEIR TENT UP FIRST?

HIKING

CAMPFIRE STORIES

CAMPFIRE SINGSONGS

FISHING CONTESTS

INDEPENDENCE DAY CELEBRATION

(Celebrated on July 4 every year.)

Independence Day is a celebration of the signing of the Declaration of Independence which was adopted by Congress on July 4, 1776. This is a celebration of the fifty-six members of the Continental Congress, who signed the Declaration of Independence and made Independence Day a reality for the United States of America.

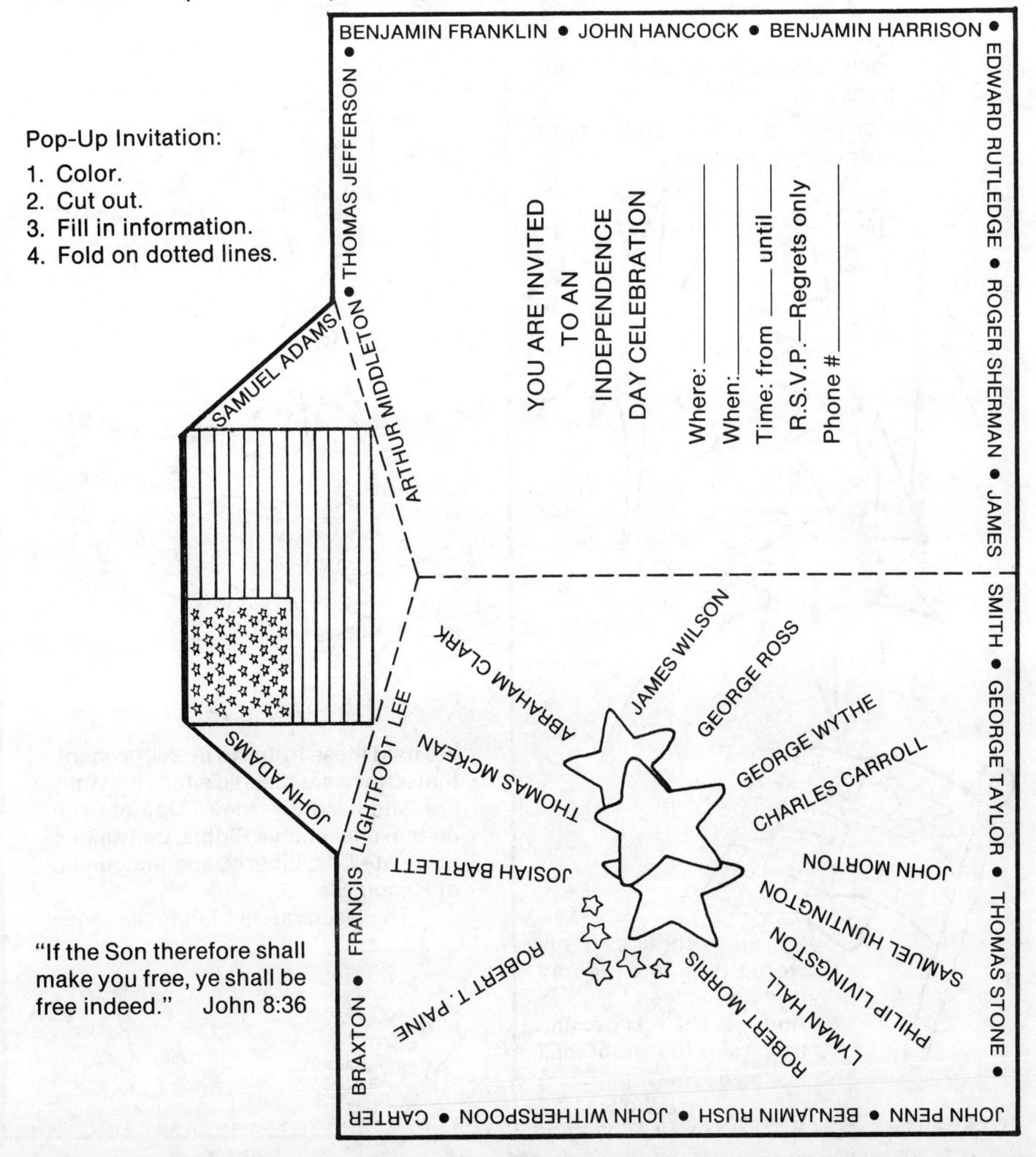

Pop-Up Invitation:
1. Color.
2. Cut out.
3. Fill in information.
4. Fold on dotted lines.

YOU ARE INVITED TO AN INDEPENDENCE DAY CELEBRATION

Where: _____
When: _____
Time: from ___ until ___
R.S.V.P.—Regrets only
Phone # _____

BENJAMIN FRANKLIN • JOHN HANCOCK • BENJAMIN HARRISON • EDWARD RUTLEDGE • ROGER SHERMAN • JAMES SMITH • GEORGE TAYLOR • THOMAS STONE • JOHN PENN • BENJAMIN RUSH • JOHN WITHERSPOON • CARTER BRAXTON • ROBERT T. PAINE • ROBERT MORRIS • LYMAN HALL • PHILIP LIVINGSTON • SAMUEL HUNTINGTON • JOHN MORTON • CHARLES CARROLL • GEORGE WYTHE • GEORGE ROSS • JAMES WILSON • ABRAHAM CLARK • THOMAS McKEAN • JOSIAH BARTLETT • FRANCIS LIGHTFOOT LEE • JOHN ADAMS • SAMUEL ADAMS • THOMAS JEFFERSON • ARTHUR MIDDLETON

"If the Son therefore shall make you free, ye shall be free indeed." John 8:36

A DOOR POSTER DECORATION

Background: white paper

Flag: red, white and blue paper

Happy Birthday Blasts: bright yellow paper

Firecrackers: bright red paper

Write the name of a signer of the Declaration of Independence on each firecracker (see state patterns for names).

Tape or glue each piece to the door according to diagram.

"..., If ye continue in my word, then are ye my disciples indeed; And ye shall know the truth, and the truth shall make you free."

John 8:31-32

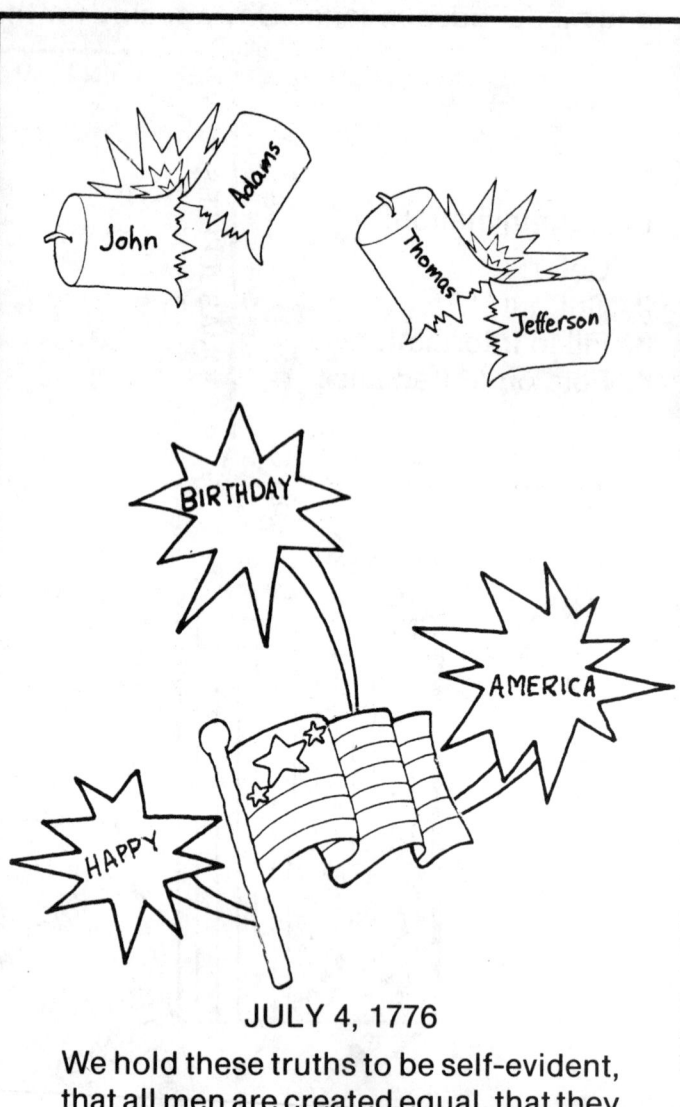

JULY 4, 1776

We hold these truths to be self-evident, that all men are created equal, that they are endowed by their Creator with certain unalienable Rights, that among these are Life, Liberty, and the pursuit of Happiness.

The Declaration of Independence

A BULLETIN BOARD DECORATION

Background: blue paper
States: white paper
Firecrackers: bright red paper
Declaration of Independence: bright yellow paper
Lettering: black marker

"Stand fast therefore in the liberty wherewith Christ hath made us free, and be not entangled again with the yoke of bondage."
Galatians 5:1

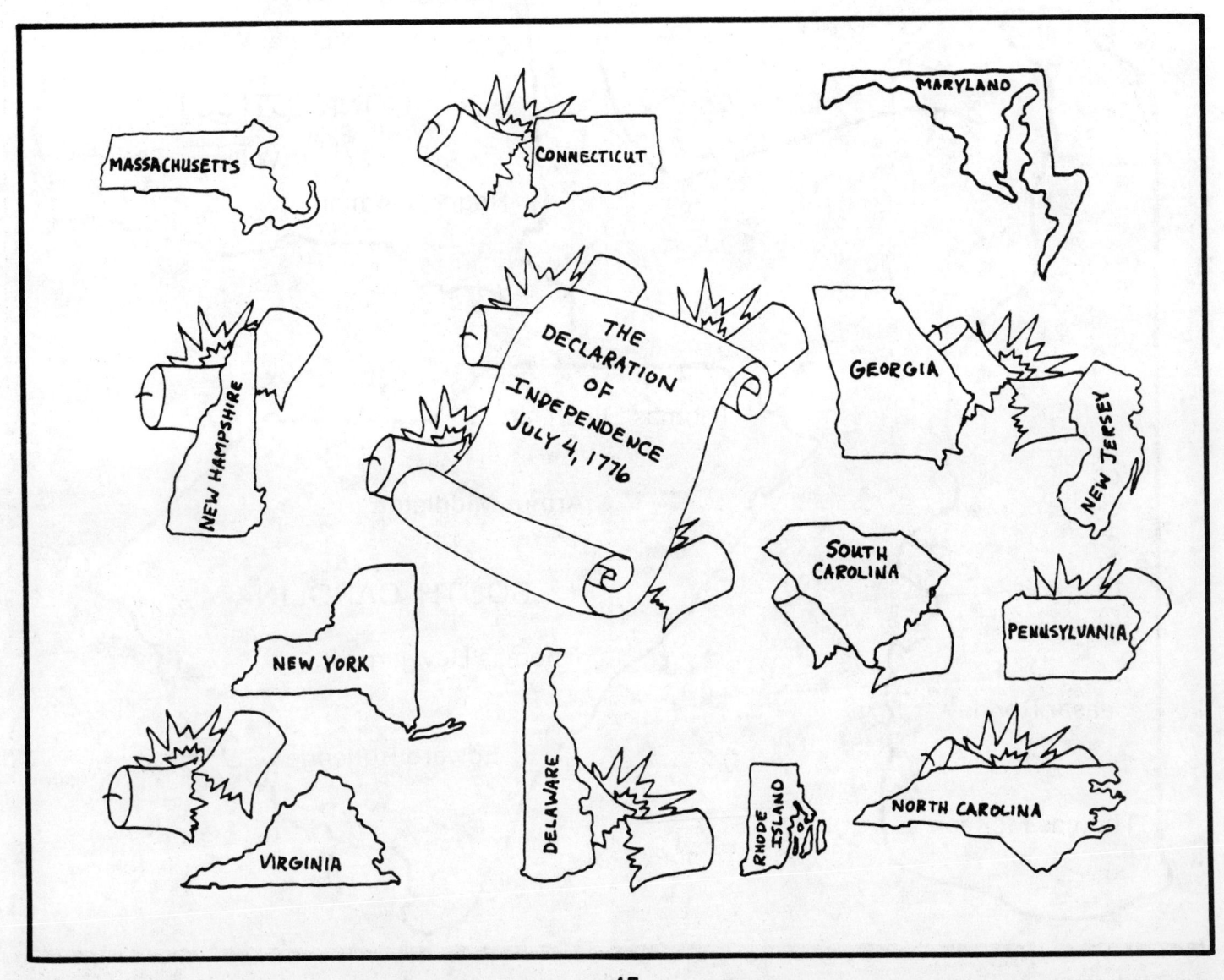

PATTERNS
FIRECRACKER AND STATES
(Showing signers of The Declaration of Independence)

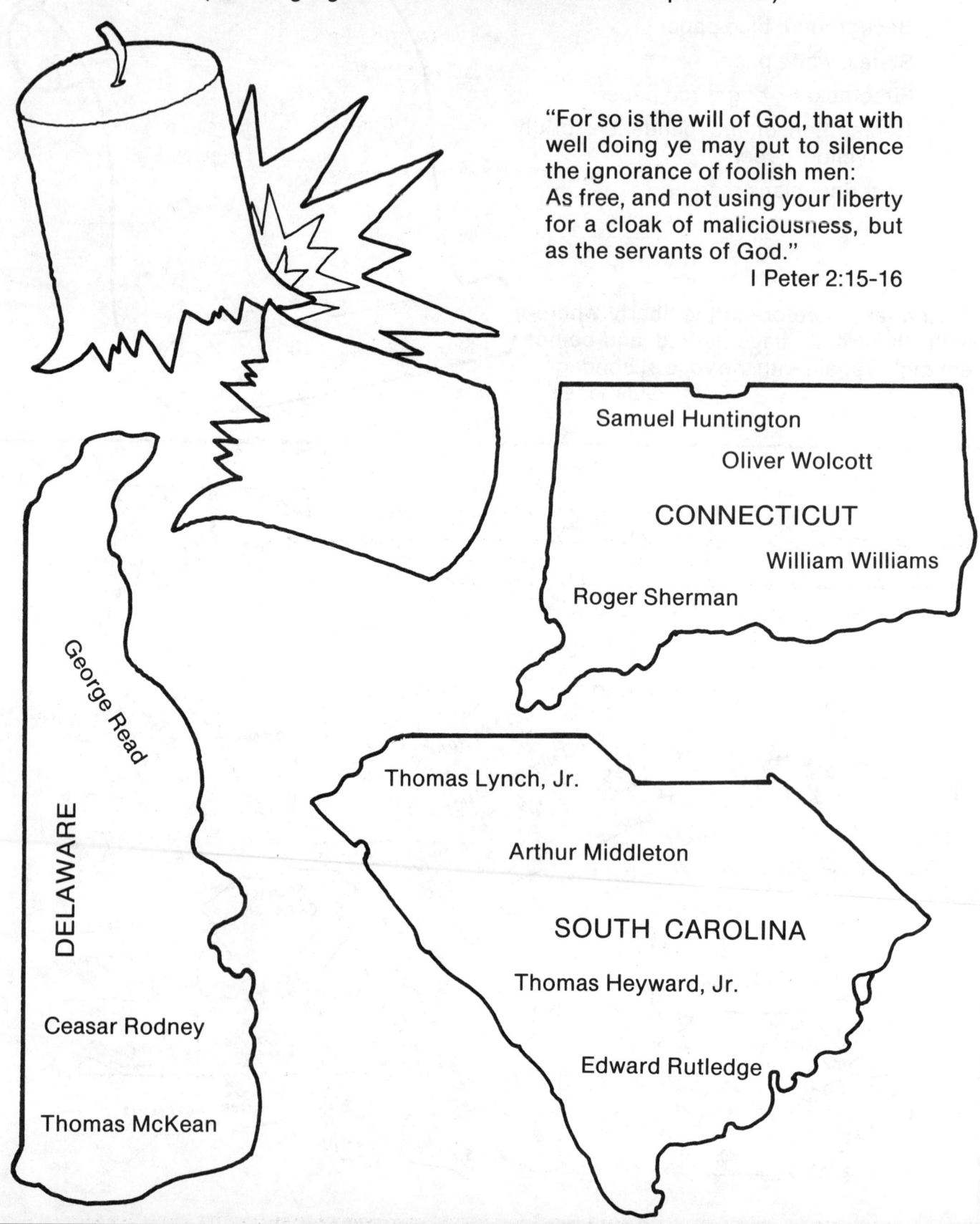

"For so is the will of God, that with well doing ye may put to silence the ignorance of foolish men: As free, and not using your liberty for a cloak of maliciousness, but as the servants of God."

I Peter 2:15-16

Samuel Huntington

Oliver Wolcott

CONNECTICUT

William Williams

Roger Sherman

George Read

DELAWARE

Ceasar Rodney

Thomas McKean

Thomas Lynch, Jr.

Arthur Middleton

SOUTH CAROLINA

Thomas Heyward, Jr.

Edward Rutledge

PATTERNS
(Showing signers of The Declaration of Independence)

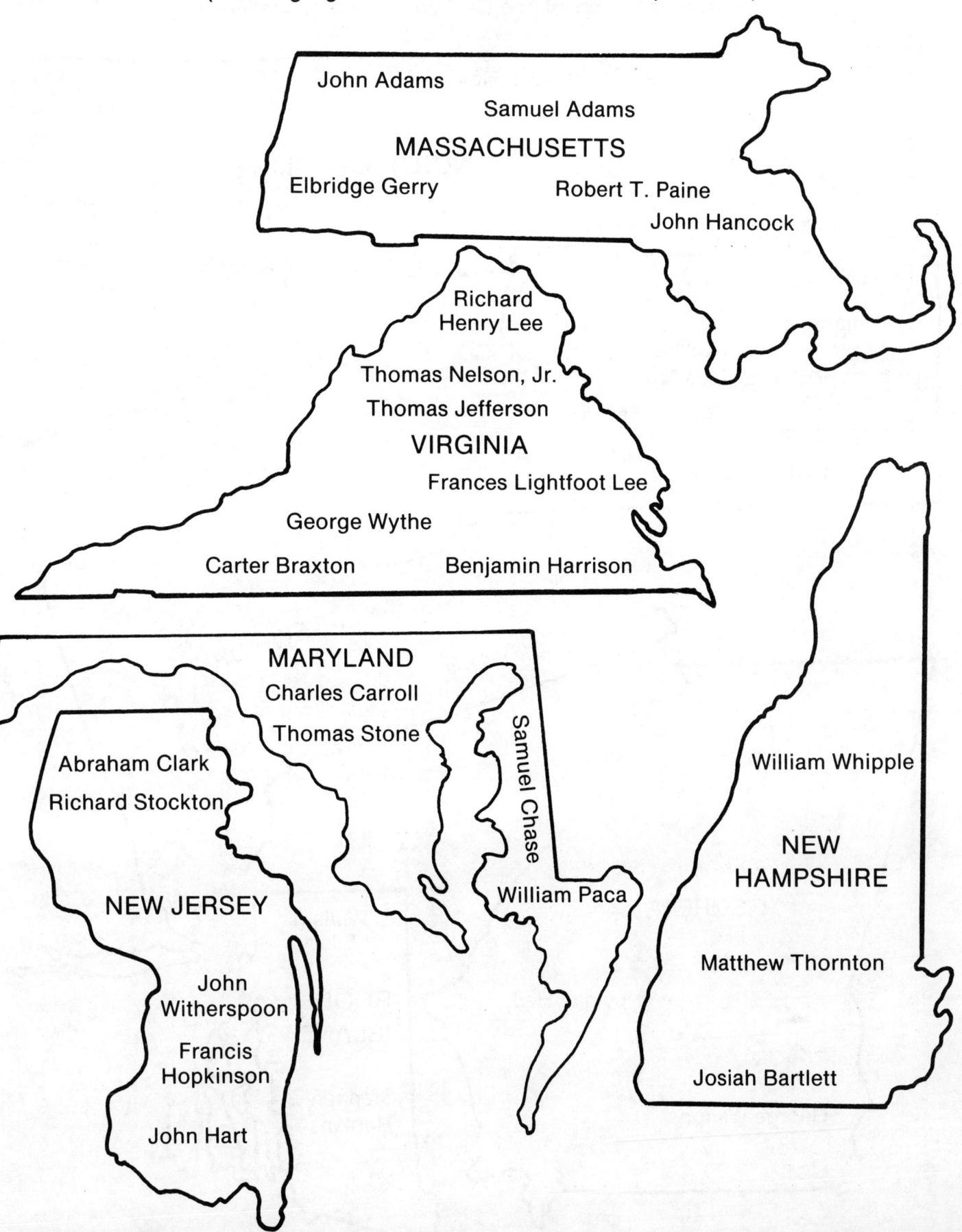

MASSACHUSETTS
- John Adams
- Samuel Adams
- Elbridge Gerry
- Robert T. Paine
- John Hancock

VIRGINIA
- Richard Henry Lee
- Thomas Nelson, Jr.
- Thomas Jefferson
- Frances Lightfoot Lee
- George Wythe
- Carter Braxton
- Benjamin Harrison

MARYLAND
- Charles Carroll
- Thomas Stone
- Samuel Chase
- William Paca

NEW JERSEY
- Abraham Clark
- Richard Stockton
- John Witherspoon
- Francis Hopkinson
- John Hart

NEW HAMPSHIRE
- William Whipple
- Matthew Thornton
- Josiah Bartlett

PATTERNS
(Showing signers of The Declaration of Independence)

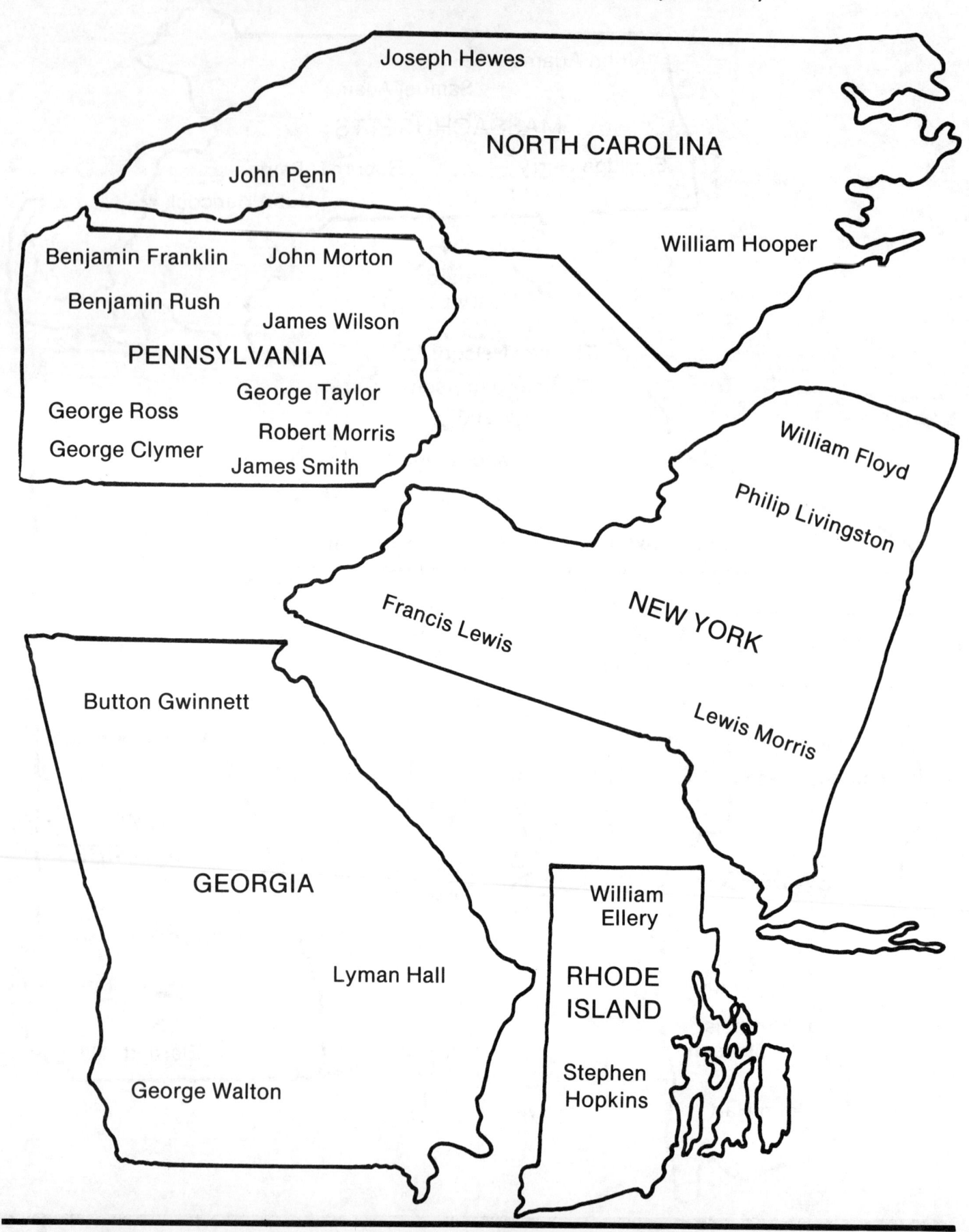

NORTH CAROLINA
- Joseph Hewes
- John Penn
- William Hooper

PENNSYLVANIA
- Benjamin Franklin
- John Morton
- Benjamin Rush
- James Wilson
- George Taylor
- George Ross
- Robert Morris
- George Clymer
- James Smith

NEW YORK
- William Floyd
- Philip Livingston
- Francis Lewis
- Lewis Morris

GEORGIA
- Button Gwinnett
- Lyman Hall
- George Walton

RHODE ISLAND
- William Ellery
- Stephen Hopkins

INDEPENDENCE DAY SPEECHES

In 1776 Independence Day was celebrated with music, bells, fireworks, parades, games, sports, shows and speeches. Reenact those early days with a lively celebration. Shout for America! Ring bells! Make joyful noise! Write and deliver lively speeches in celebration of Independence Day!

Sugggestions: INDEPENDENCE—Then, now, and forever; Franklin, Jefferson, Adams and others; Freedom for All; Shout Out for America.

Title of Speech:_____

_____
_____
_____
_____
_____
_____
_____
_____
_____
_____
_____
_____

Written by: _____

". . . Christ hath made us free, . . ." Galatians 5:1

BUMPER STICKERS

Shout out for America by taping the "bumper stickers" to cars, doors, windows, notebooks, etc.

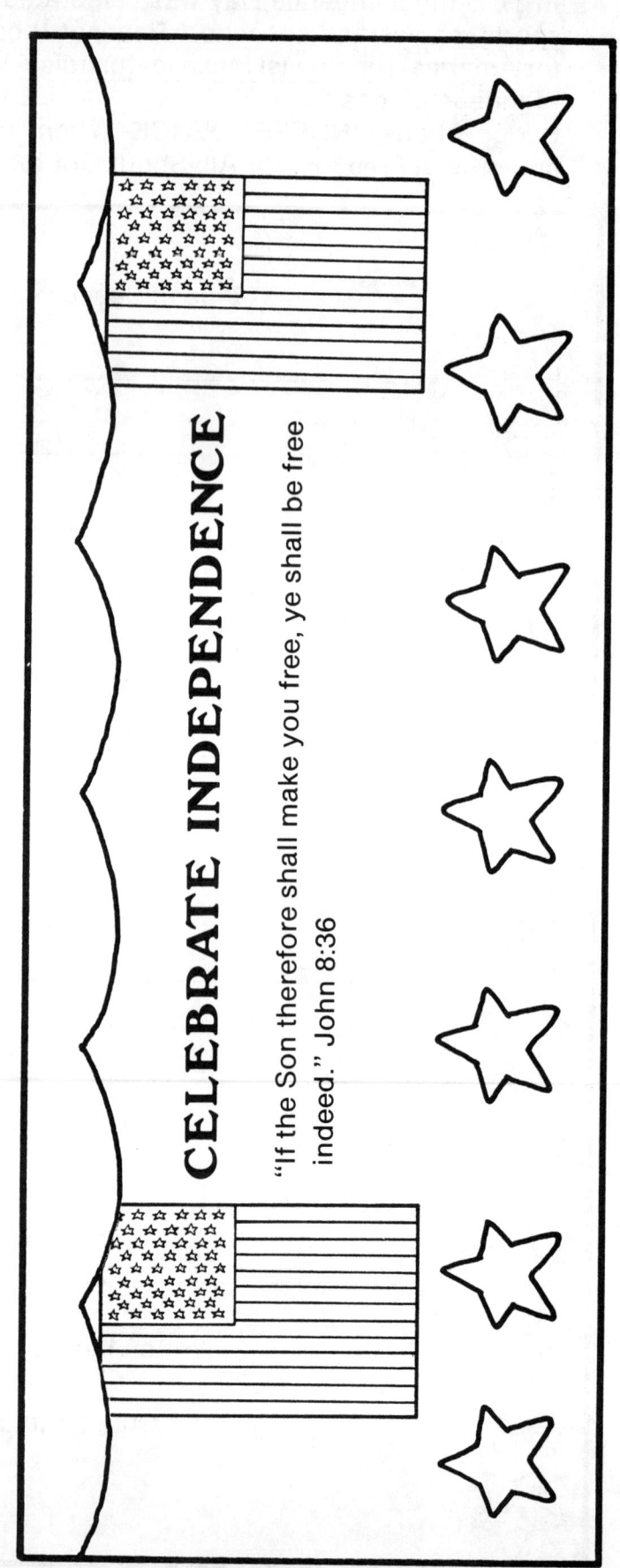

"CHRIST HATH MADE US FREE"
Galatians 5:1

CELEBRATE INDEPENDENCE
"If the Son therefore shall make you free, ye shall be free indeed." John 8:36

ANGEL FOOD DELIGHT

Slice one cooled angel food cake into three sections horizontally and set aside.

Dissolve 3-oz. package of strawberry gelatin in 1½ cups boiling water.

Add 8-oz. package frozen strawberries.

Chill until set.

Stir gelatin and fold in 1 cup whipped cream.

Place bottom third of cake on a cake platter.

Spread ½ strawberry mix over bottom section of cake.

Place middle section of cake over bottom section.

Spread the other half of strawberry mixture over middle section.

Place top section of cake over middle section.

Top cake with another 1 to 1½ cups of whipped cream.

Slice and serve immediately.

"... there is joy in the presence of the angels of God over one sinner that repenteth." Luke 15:10

A CIRCUS CELEBRATION

(Honoring P.T. Barnum, born July 5, 1810. Barnum started his famous circus which is known today as the Ringling Brothers and Barnum & Bailey Circus in 1871.)

Have the older children entertain the younger children with a Big Top Circus!

Invitation:
1. Color. 2. Cut out. 3. Fill in information. 4. Hand out to the younger children.

"The Lord hath done great things for us; whereof we are glad."

Psalm 126:3

CIRCUS

Where: _____

When: _____

Time: from _____ until _____

You are invited!

CIRCUS COSTUMES

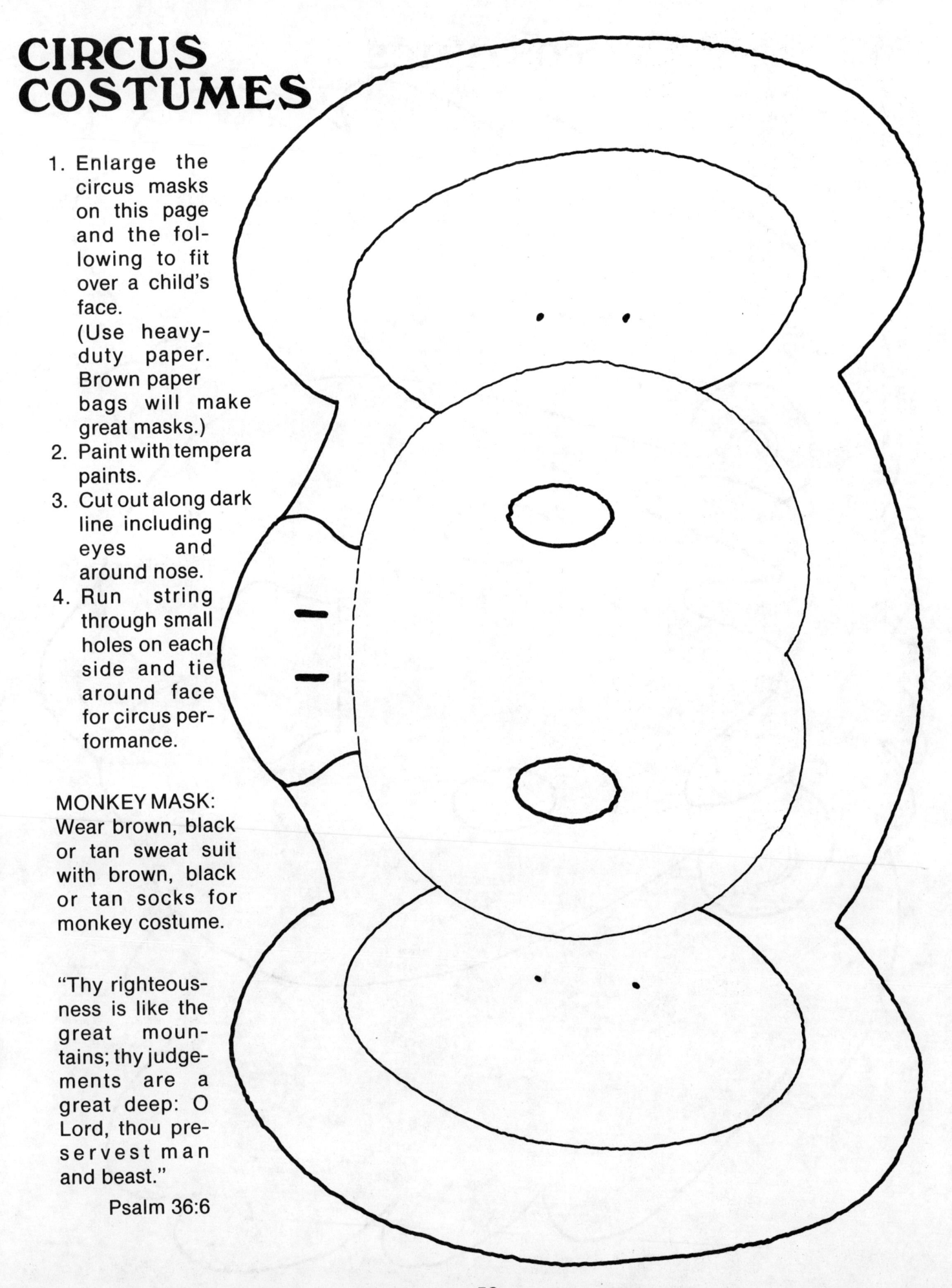

1. Enlarge the circus masks on this page and the following to fit over a child's face.
   (Use heavy-duty paper. Brown paper bags will make great masks.)
2. Paint with tempera paints.
3. Cut out along dark line including eyes and around nose.
4. Run string through small holes on each side and tie around face for circus performance.

MONKEY MASK: Wear brown, black or tan sweat suit with brown, black or tan socks for monkey costume.

"Thy righteousness is like the great mountains; thy judgements are a great deep: O Lord, thou preservest man and beast."

Psalm 36:6

COSTUMES

LION MASK: Wear yellow or gold sweat suit with same color socks for lion costume.

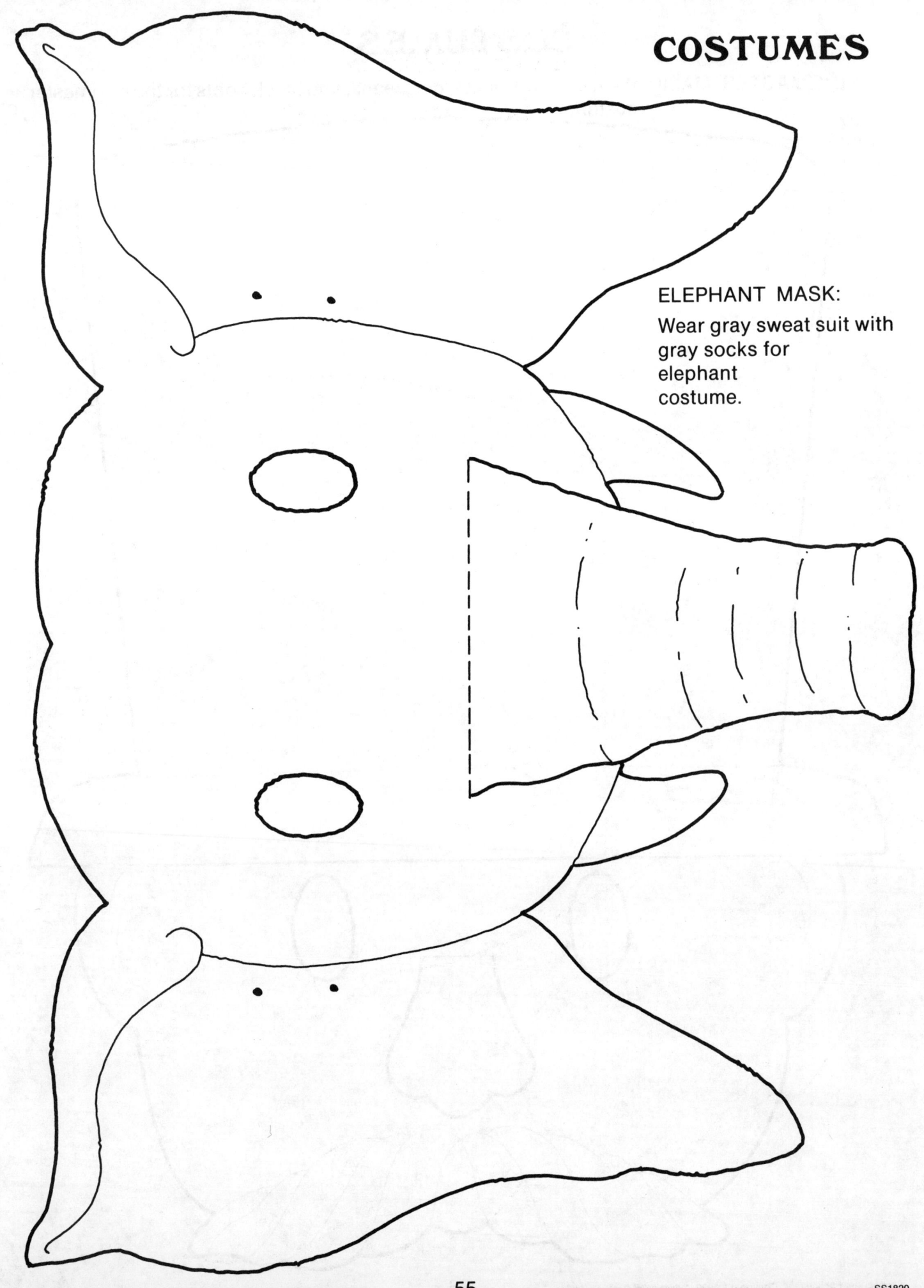

COSTUMES

ELEPHANT MASK:
Wear gray sweat suit with gray socks for elephant costume.

55

Shining Star Publications, Copyright © 1990, A division of Good Apple, Inc.

SS1820

COSTUMES

RINGMASTER MASK: Wear colorful jacket, blue jeans, and black boots for the ringmaster costume.

CLOWN MASK:

Wear brightly colored sweat suit. (Mix and match the colors.) Add fluffy house shoes and white gloves.

COSTUMES

Shining Star Publications, Copyright © 1990, A division of Good Apple, Inc.

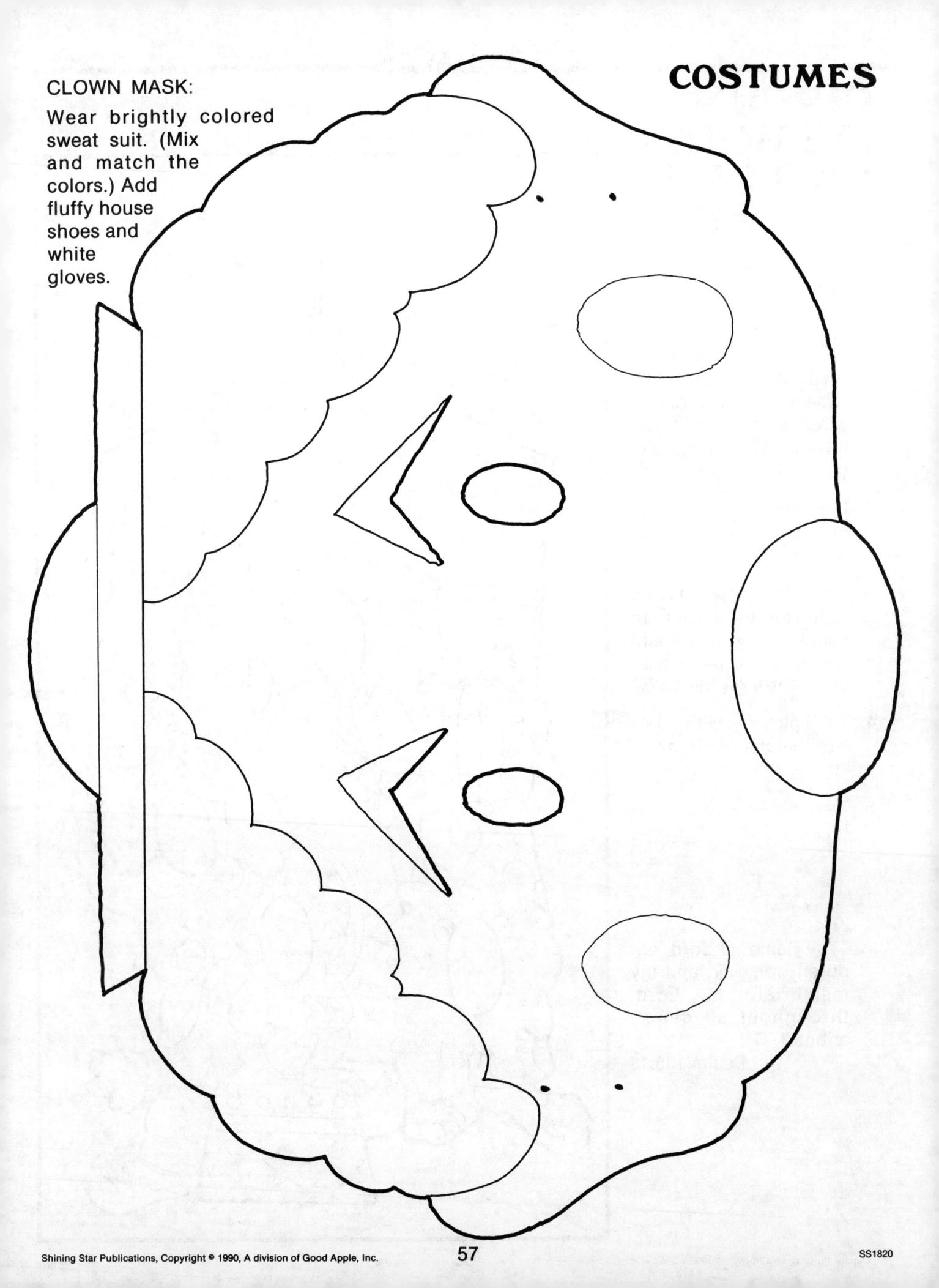

SS1820

CIRCUS MEMORY PICTURE FRAME

1. Reproduce the circus scene shown on a 4' × 6' piece of heavy cardboard. Cut circles out to allow faces to show through for pictures. (Use a thin piece of plywood same size if you have a saw that will cut circles.)

2. Paint picture poster with brightly colored tempera paints.

3. When completed, ask six children at a time to stand behind cardboard scene and to place their faces through the holes.

4. Take pictures with a Polaroid camera, if available.

5. Tack pictures to a bulletin board for all to see.

"Thy name, O Lord, endureth for ever; and thy memorial, O Lord, throughout all generations."

Psalm 135:13

POP-THE-BALLOON BOOTH

Locate a heavy cardboard refrigerator box. (Try a local appliance store.) Cut a window on the front side and a small door on the back side. See diagram.

Paint the outside of the box with white paint. Let dry. Use brightly colored paint to scatter polka dots over white. Or splatter paint white box with brightly colored paints.

Enlarge and reproduce the clown patterns provided on the following page. Color, cut out and glue to the inside back wall through the window on the front side.

Blow up small balloons and tape to the nose area of each clown.

Tape a line across the floor 3-4 feet away from the window. Allow each child three tries to throw a dart and pop the balloons.

Award appropriate prizes for one, two, or three ballons popped.

Other ideas: The same booth could be used for:

RING TOSS GAME
Place hooks on inside wall. Toss small rings and try to hook the ring.

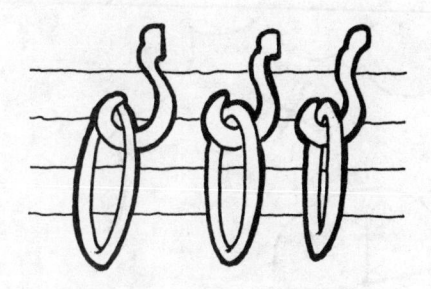

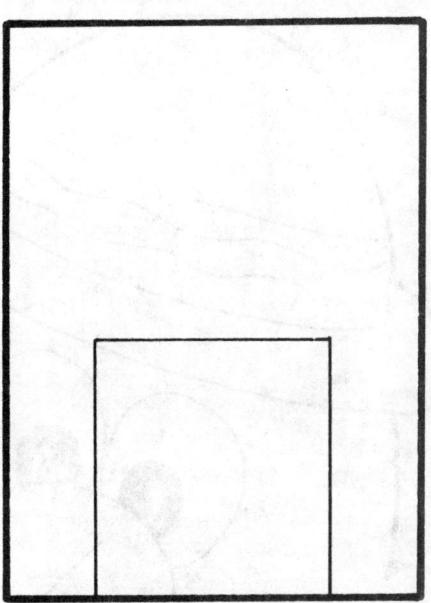

TENNIS BALL BOWL
Lay box on its side. Line up plastic bottles along one end. Bowl tennis ball to see how many bottles will be knocked down.

PUPPET BOOTH
Make circus puppets from old socks and scrap materials. Have two to three children at a time crawl inside door of box and perform a puppet show through the window.

Shining Star Publications, Copyright © 1990, A division of Good Apple, Inc.

Clown Patterns for POP-THE-BALLOON BOOTH

1. Enlarge and reproduce.

2. Color with brightly colored markers.

3. Cut out.

4. Glue on the inside back wall of booth.

5. Tape balloon to the nose area of each clown.

CIRCUS ICE-CREAM CONES

Allow the children to build their own!

Supply cones and ice cream along with gumdrops, red hots, raisins, coconut colored from food coloring, whipped cream, icing in decorator cans, hard candies, etc.

Encourage the children to be creative and think circus!

eyes: gumdrops

hair: red icing

mouth: whipping cream

hat: black construction paper

hair: colored coconut

eyes: chocolate chips

smile: red icing

mane: yellow icing

eyes and nose: raisins

teeth: red hots

CELEBRATE HAWAII

(Hawaii became our 50th state on August 21, 1959.)

"One thing have I desired of the Lord, that will I seek after; that I may dwell in the house of the Lord all the days of my life, to behold the beauty of the Lord, and to inquire in his temple."

Psalm 27:4

Invitation: 1. Color the Hawaiian shirt with brightly colored markers. 2. Cut out along dark line. 3. Fill in information. 4. Hand out to guests.

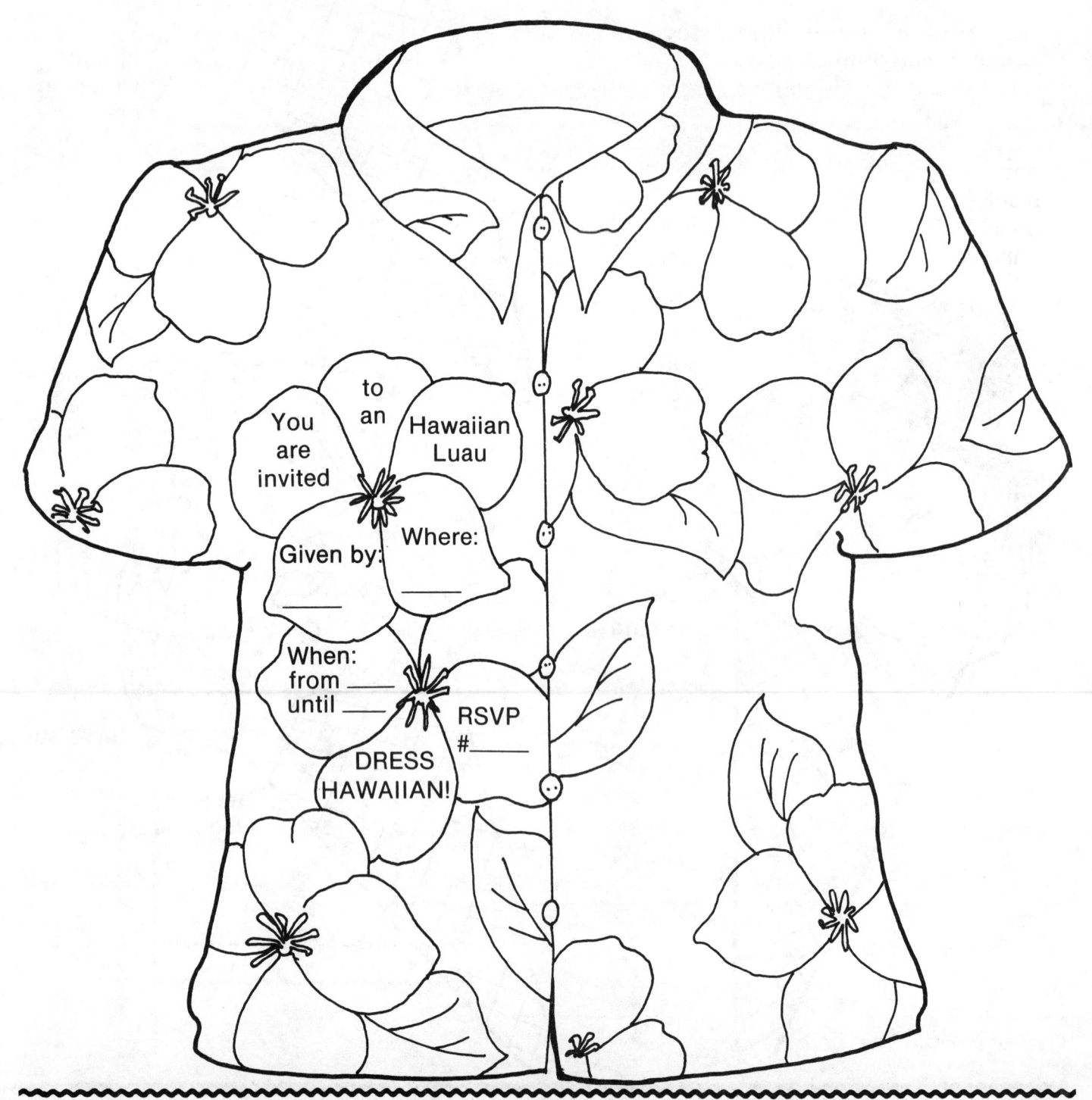

You are invited to an Hawaiian Luau

Given by: ____

Where: ____

When: from ____ until ____

RSVP #____

DRESS HAWAIIAN!

DECORATIONS FOR HAWAIIAN LUAU

Part of decorating for a luau is selecting the right location for the party. If possible, choose a patio area outside. Or if practical for your group, choose a backyard swimming pool area. Be sure to have enough adult supervision so as to be safe with the swimming.

For decoration surround the area with "homemade" trees native to Hawaii. Use the following patterns to make banana trees and poinciana flowering trees.

To make the tree trunks for the banana and poinciana flowering trees:
1. Collect the cardboard center rolls from carpet stores.

2. Spray paint each roll with green paint.

3. Let dry.

(Cut cardboard rolls to make different size trees.) →

To make the stand for each tree:
1. Collect 4 blocks of wood—2" thick and 12" long.

2. Nail together snugly around bottom end of each tree trunk to make tree stand.

See following pages for banana leaf patterns and poinciana flower patterns.

Shining Star Publications, Copyright © 1990, A division of Good Apple, Inc.   63   SS1820

BANANA LEAF

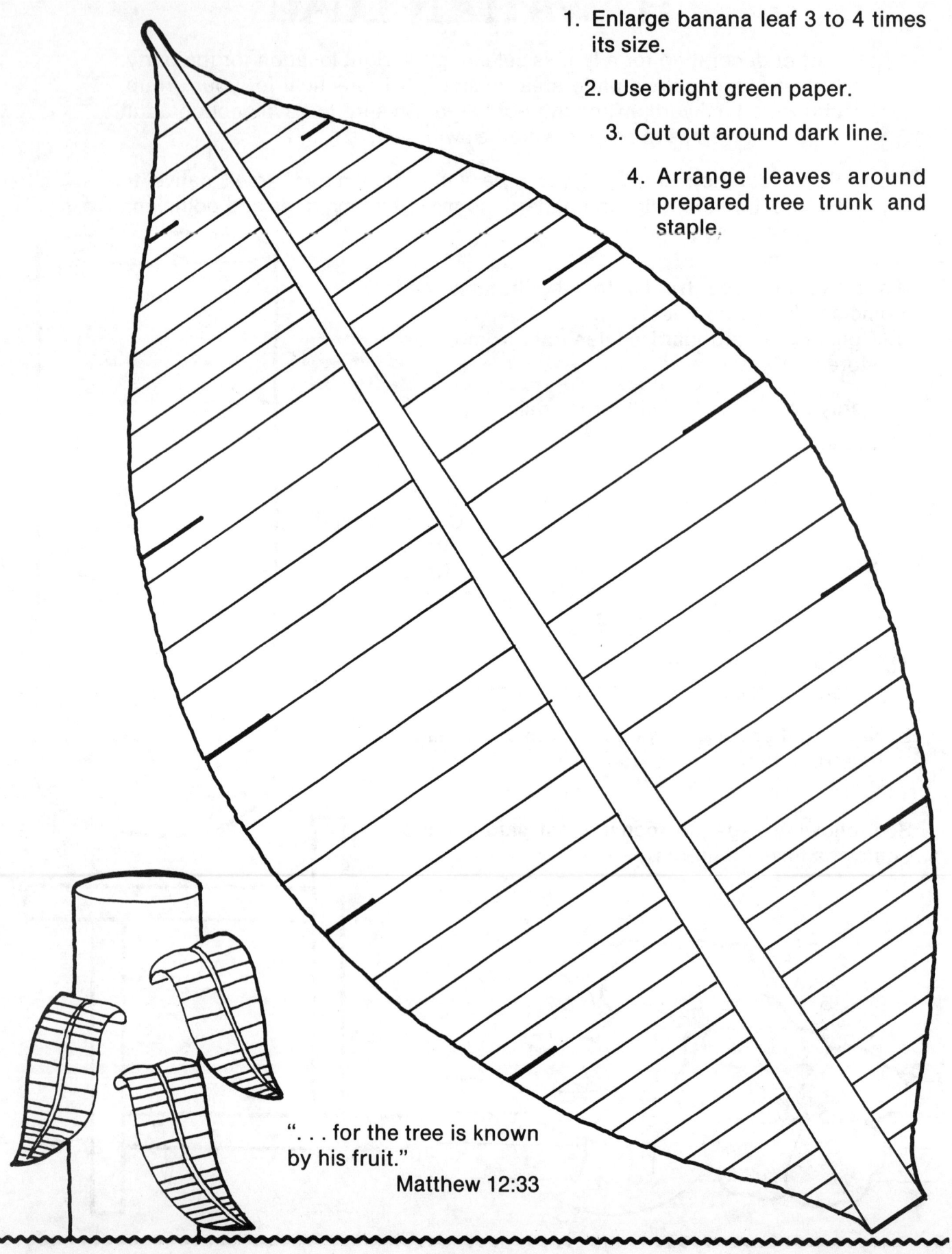

1. Enlarge banana leaf 3 to 4 times its size.
2. Use bright green paper.
3. Cut out around dark line.
4. Arrange leaves around prepared tree trunk and staple.

". . . for the tree is known by his fruit."

Matthew 12:33

BANANAS

1. Enlarge bananas 2 to 3 times the size of the pattern.
2. Use a bright yellow paper and outline with black marker.
3. Reproduce 2 patterns for each bunch of bananas.
4. Staple around edges and stuff with tissue to make three-dimensional.
5. Then arrange bananas around tree trunk and staple.

Note: Bananas grow up, not hanging down on a banana tree.

"But the fruit of the Spirit is love, joy, peace, longsuffering, gentleness, goodness, faith, Meekness, temperance: against such there is no law."
Galatians 5:22-23

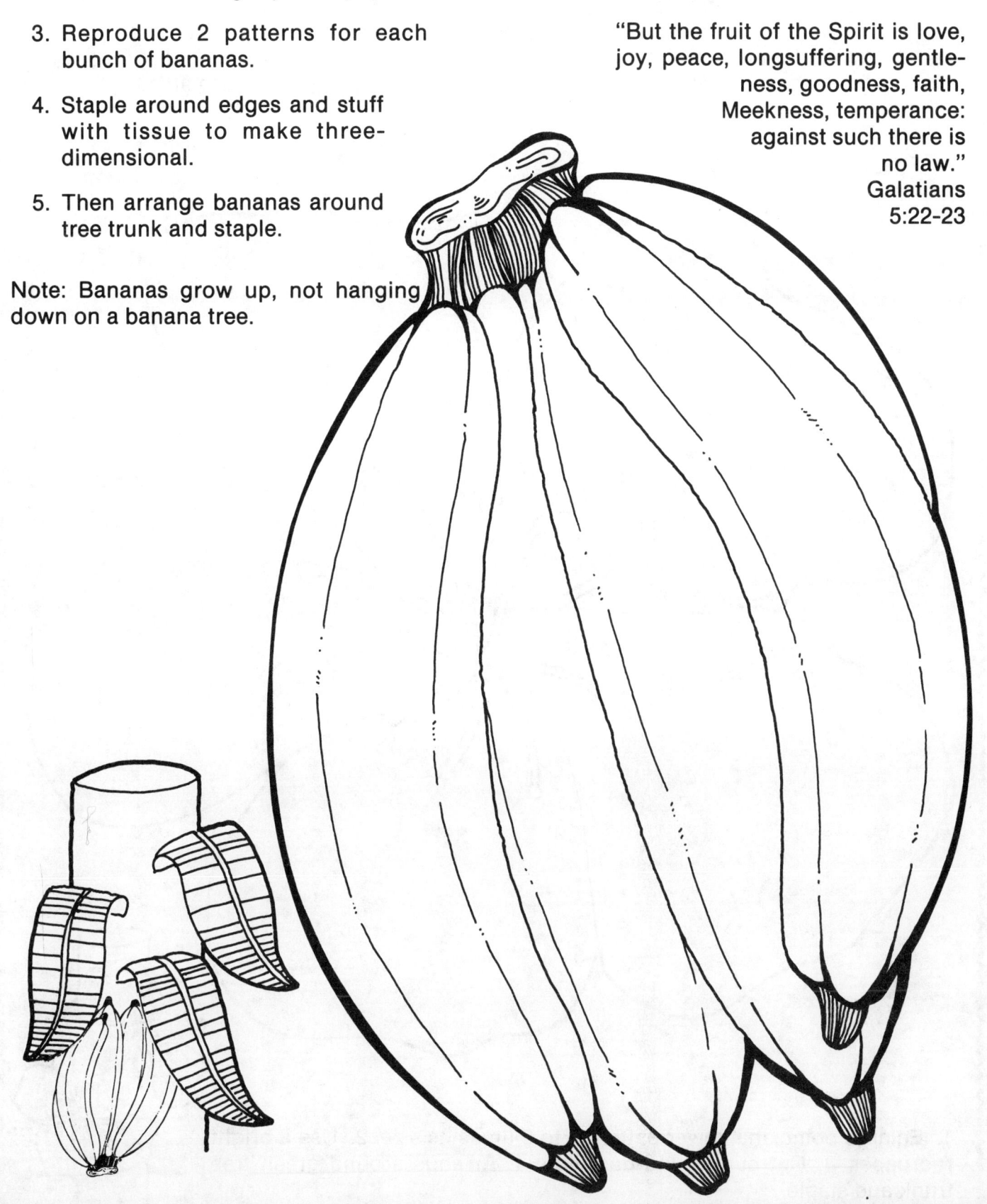

POINCIANA

(The poinciana is a flowering tree. The poinciana flower has five red petals, one of which is dotted with yellow. The flower also holds ten long stamens in its center.)

"The grass withereth, the flower fadeth: but the word of our God shall stand for ever."

Isaiah 40:8

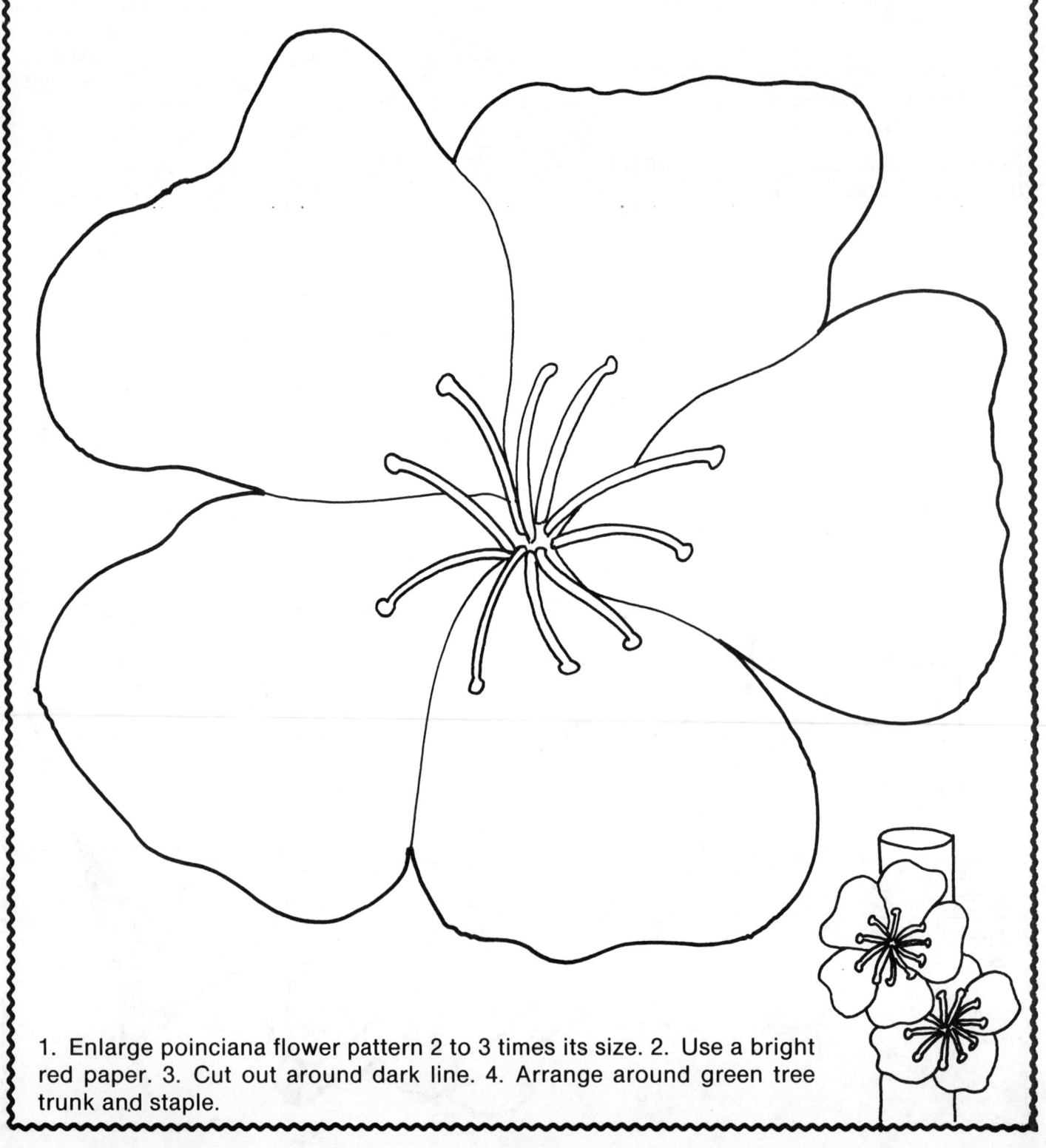

1. Enlarge poinciana flower pattern 2 to 3 times its size. 2. Use a bright red paper. 3. Cut out around dark line. 4. Arrange around green tree trunk and staple.

LUAU FAVOR: LEI

A lei is a wreath made by stringing flowers together and is very popular in the Hawaiian Islands.

To make a lei for your celebration:

1. Reproduce enough of the flower patterns provided to make a lei for each guest.

2. Use brightly colored paper.

3. Use colored string. (Length- 1 yard each.)

4. Color macaroni with food colorings and string one piece of macaroni between each flower.

5. Tie off and place around each guest's neck as they arrive to Celebrate Hawaii!

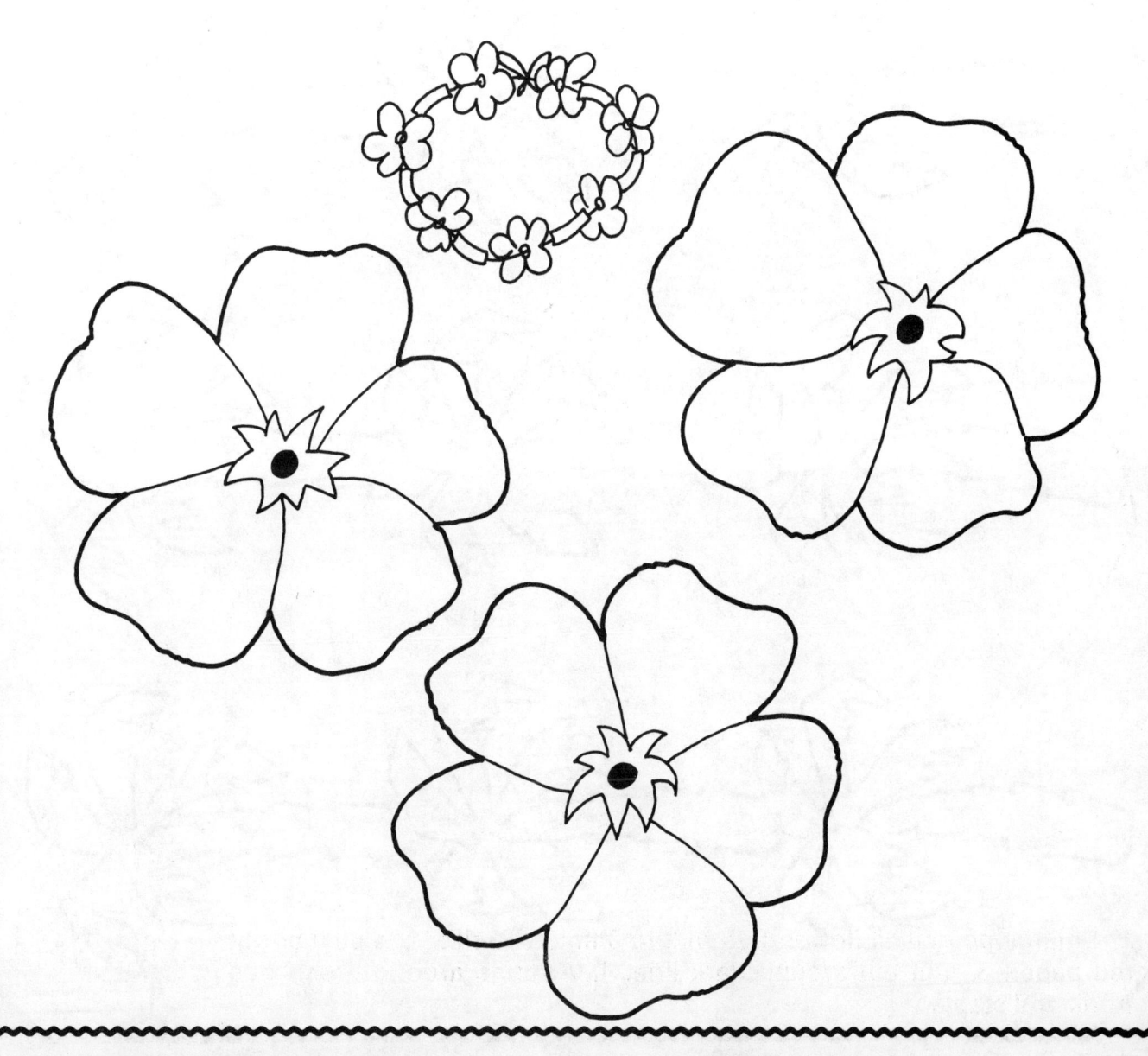

PLACE MAT FOR LUAU
1. Reproduce one for every guest. 2. Color with bright markers.

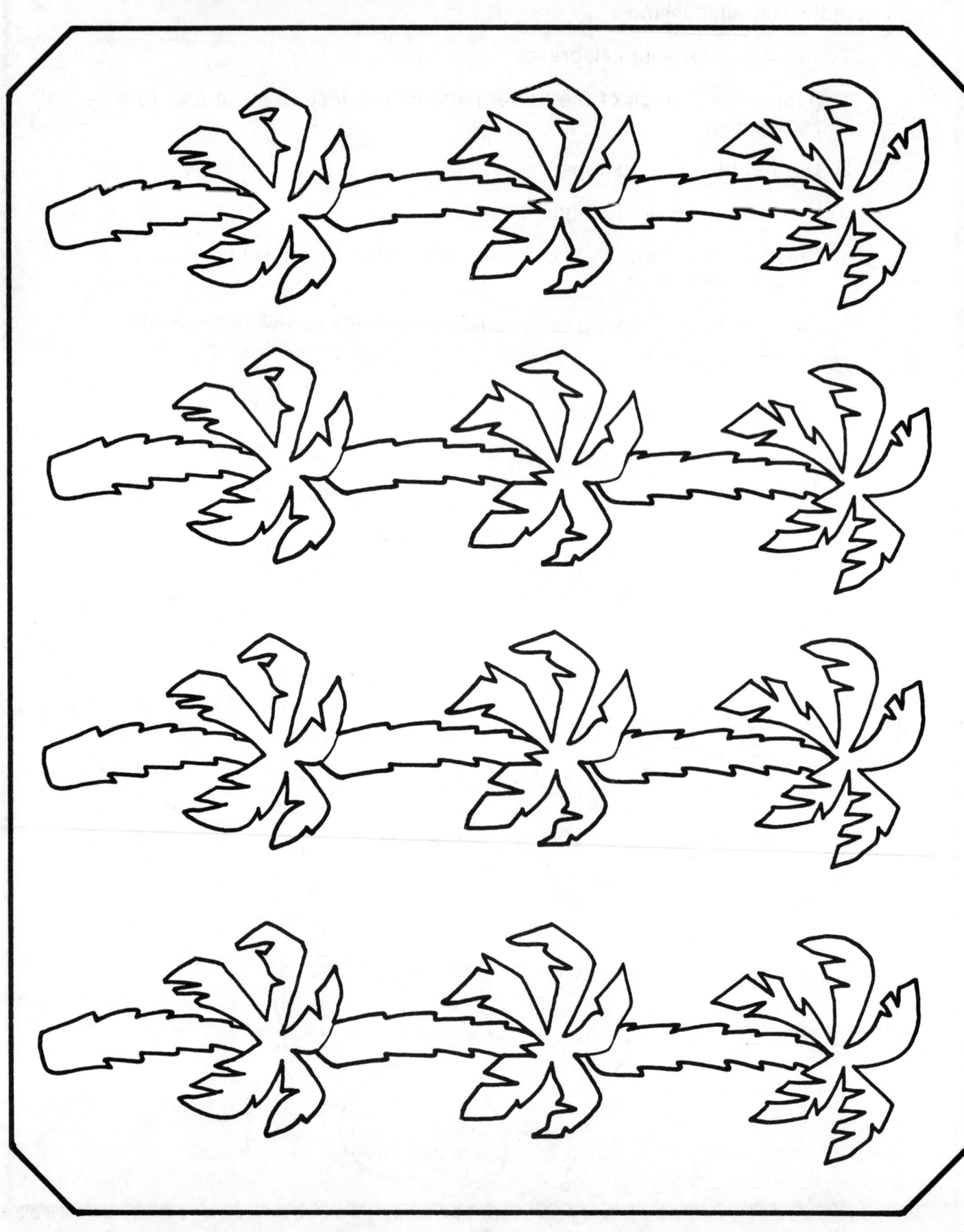

TOOTHPICK AND STRAW DECORATIONS

Reproduce the palm tree patterns provided. Use to decorate toothpicks. Stick toothpicks into bite-sized chunks of pineapple and bananas for party snacks.

Or use to decorate straws for party beverages.

Try and recite the Hawaiian Lord's Prayer before eating the Luau feast.

THE LORD'S PRAYER
In English and Hawaiian

E ko makou makua iloko o ka lani,
Our Father which art in heaven,

E hoanoia kou inoa
Hallowed be Thy name.

E hiki mai kou aupuni;
Thy kingdom come.

E malamaia kou makemake ma ka honua nei,
Thy will be done on earth,

E like me ia i malamaia ma ka lani la.
As it is in heaven.

E haawi mai ia makou i keia la, i ai na makou no neia la.
Give us this day our daily bread.

E kala mai hoi ia makou, i ka makou lawehala ana,
And forgive us our debts,

Me makou e kala nei i ka poe i lawehala i ka makou.
As we forgive our debtors.

Mai hookuu oe ia makou i ka hoowalewale ia mai
And lead us not into temptation,

E hoopakele no nae ia makou i ka ino;
But deliver us from evil;

No ka mea, nou ke aupuni
For thine is the kingdom

A me ka mana, a me ka hoonaniia, a mau loa, aku, Amene.
And the power, and the glory, forever. Amen.

HAWAIIAN WORDS PUZZLE

Duplicate one puzzle sheet for each guest. Instruct the guests to read the Hawaiian words and their definitions. Then see how many words each guest can locate and circle on the puzzle.

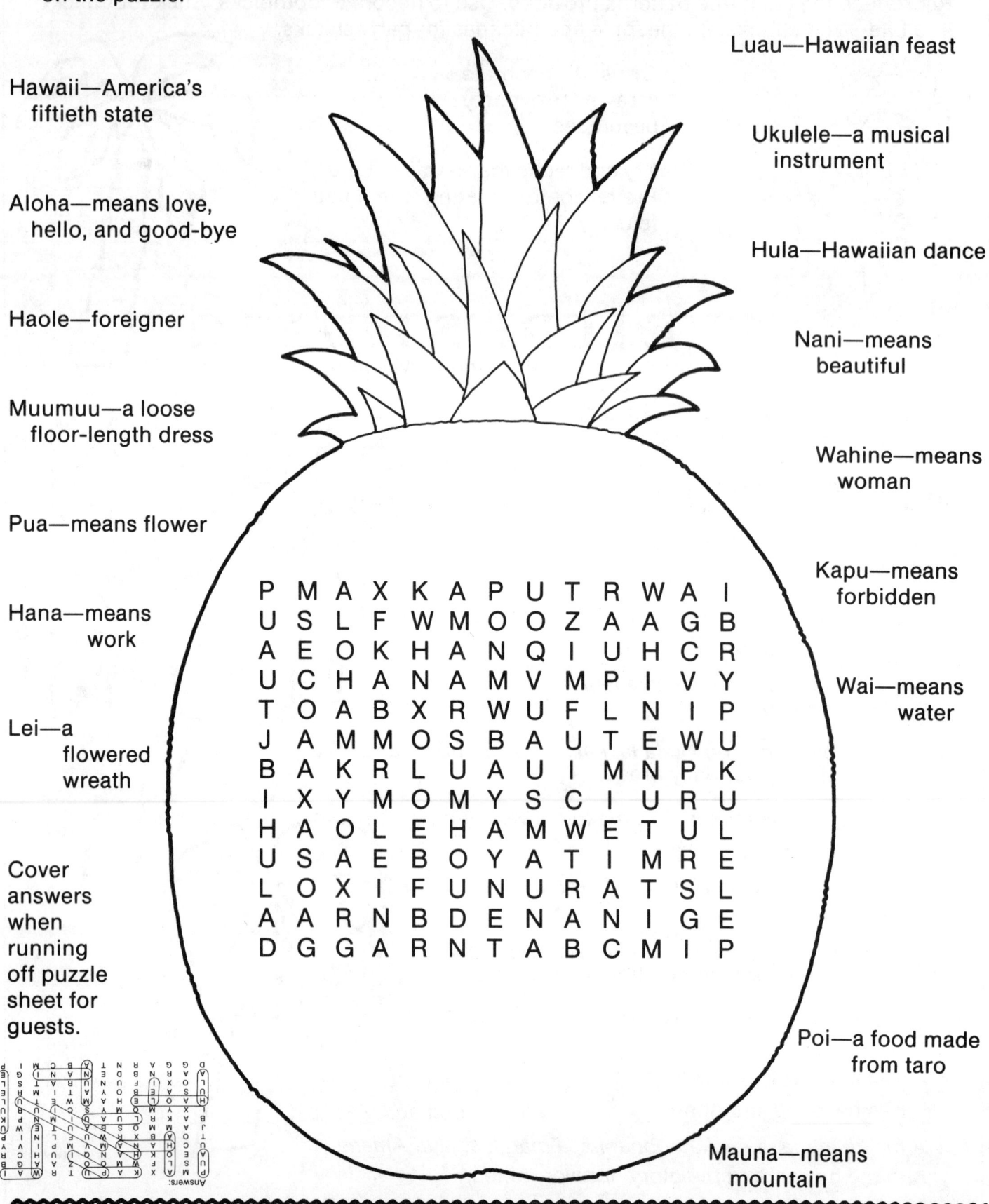

Hawaii—America's fiftieth state

Aloha—means love, hello, and good-bye

Haole—foreigner

Muumuu—a loose floor-length dress

Pua—means flower

Hana—means work

Lei—a flowered wreath

Cover answers when running off puzzle sheet for guests.

Luau—Hawaiian feast

Ukulele—a musical instrument

Hula—Hawaiian dance

Nani—means beautiful

Wahine—means woman

Kapu—means forbidden

Wai—means water

Poi—a food made from taro

Mauna—means mountain

```
P M A X K A P U T R W A I
U S L F W M O O Z A A G B
A E O K H A N Q I U H C R
U C H A N A M V M P I V Y
T O A B X R W U F L N I P
J A M M O S B A U T E W U
B A K R L U A U I M N P K
I X Y M O M Y S C I U R U
H A O L E H A M W E T U L
U S A E B O Y A T I M R E
L O X I F U N U R A T S L
A A R N B D E N A N I G E
D G G A R N T A B C M I P
```

HAWAIIAN LUAU FEAST

A typical luau feast might consist of roasted pig, fish, rice, poi (a paste-like food made from the taro plant), fresh pineapple and bananas, papayas, and macadamia nuts.

For your luau celebration serve slices of cooked ham, bite-sized chunks of pineapple and bananas, slices of papaya fruit, and roasted macadamia nuts.

As a substitute for poi, make up a tapioca pudding:

Combine: 1 quart milk
½ cup tapioca
½ cup sugar
Let stand for 10 minutes.
Add 3 beaten egg yolks.
Stir and bring to boil.
Remove from heat and add 2 teaspoons vanilla.
Fold mixture into 3 beaten egg whites.
Let cool and eat.

For an "Island Beverage" combine 2 quarts of pineapple sherbert with 1½ to 2 gallons of ginger ale.

"Nevertheless he left not himself without witness, in that he did good, and gave us rain from heaven, and fruitful seasons, filling our hearts with food and gladness."

Acts 14:17

CELEBRATE THE AMERICAN RED CROSS

(Founded by Clara Barton on August 22, 1881.)

"But a certain Samaritan, as he journeyed, came where he was: and when he saw him, he had compassion on him,
And went to him, and bound up his wounds, pouring in oil and wine, and set him on his own beast, and brought him to an inn, and took care of him."

Luke 10:33-34

ANNOUNCEMENT   ANNOUNCEMENT   ANNOUNCEMENT

PLEASE COME TOGETHER TO CELEBRATE THE AMERICAN RED CROSS

founded by Clara Barton—August 22, 1881

Where: _____

When: _____

Time: from _____ until _____

1. Cut along dotted line.
2. Pin to shirt or blouse.
3. Wear to celebration.
4. Please volunteer.

PLEASE VOLUNTEER

*Please bring a "sack supper" for a needy person.
Call telephone # _____ for information.

ANNOUNCEMENT   ANNOUNCEMENT   ANNOUNCEMENT

DECORATIONS

Reproduce a minimum of 20 to 30 Red Cross/Good Samaritan flags. Leave background white and color cross red. Glue wooden dowel stick to left-hand side of each flag. Push dowel stick into ground to make flag stand. Spread flags around area where celebration is to take place.

THE GOOD SAMARITAN

Luke 10:30-37

"Go, and do thou likewise."

RED CROSS VOLUNTEER CHECKLIST

Reproduce at least five copies for every person expected to attend the Red Cross celebration. Have each one fill out a sheet for himself and pass the others to family and friends. Instruct that all the volunteer sheets be returned by a certain date to an appointed person who will be sure to turn them in to your local Red Cross office for further reference in time of need.

BE A GOOD SAMARITAN AND A RED CROSS VOLUNTEER

What can you do to be a Good Samaritan and to help the American Red Cross? For suggestions call your local Red Cross telephone number—_____

The following checklist will be turned over to the Red Cross for future reference when needed. Won't you please be a Good Samaritan by checking those things for which you are willing to volunteer?

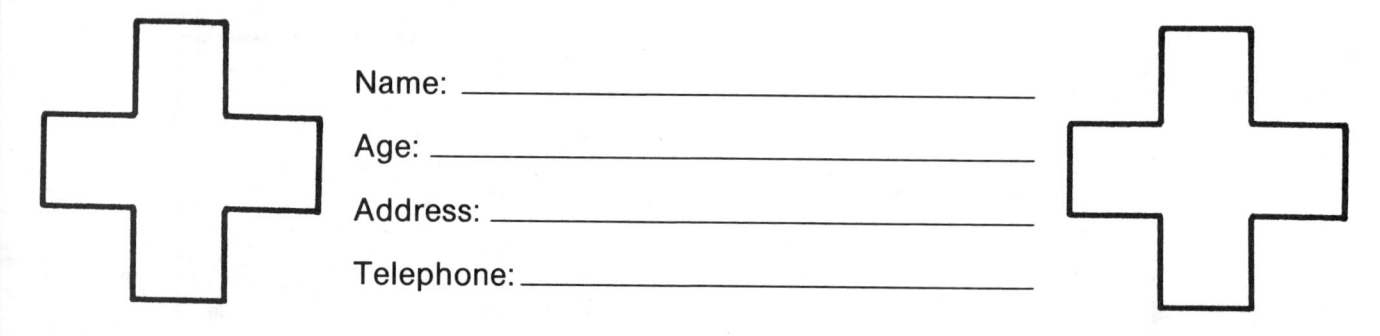

Name: _____

Age: _____

Address: _____

Telephone: _____

- ☐ participate in a canned goods drive in order to fill local food banks

- ☐ make phone calls to make people aware of Red Cross needs

- ☐ wash windows and ask for donations for Red Cross

- ☐ help repair needed shelters

- ☐ give blood or encourage parents to give blood in a Red Cross blood drive

- ☐ bake goods and work in bake sale to earn money for Red Cross

- ☐ participate in car wash to earn money for Red Cross

- ☐ participate in a clothes drive for needy families

- ☐ participate in Red Cross safety programs

Shining Star Publications, Copyright © 1990, A division of Good Apple, Inc.

SS1820

RED CROSS DONATION ENVELOPE

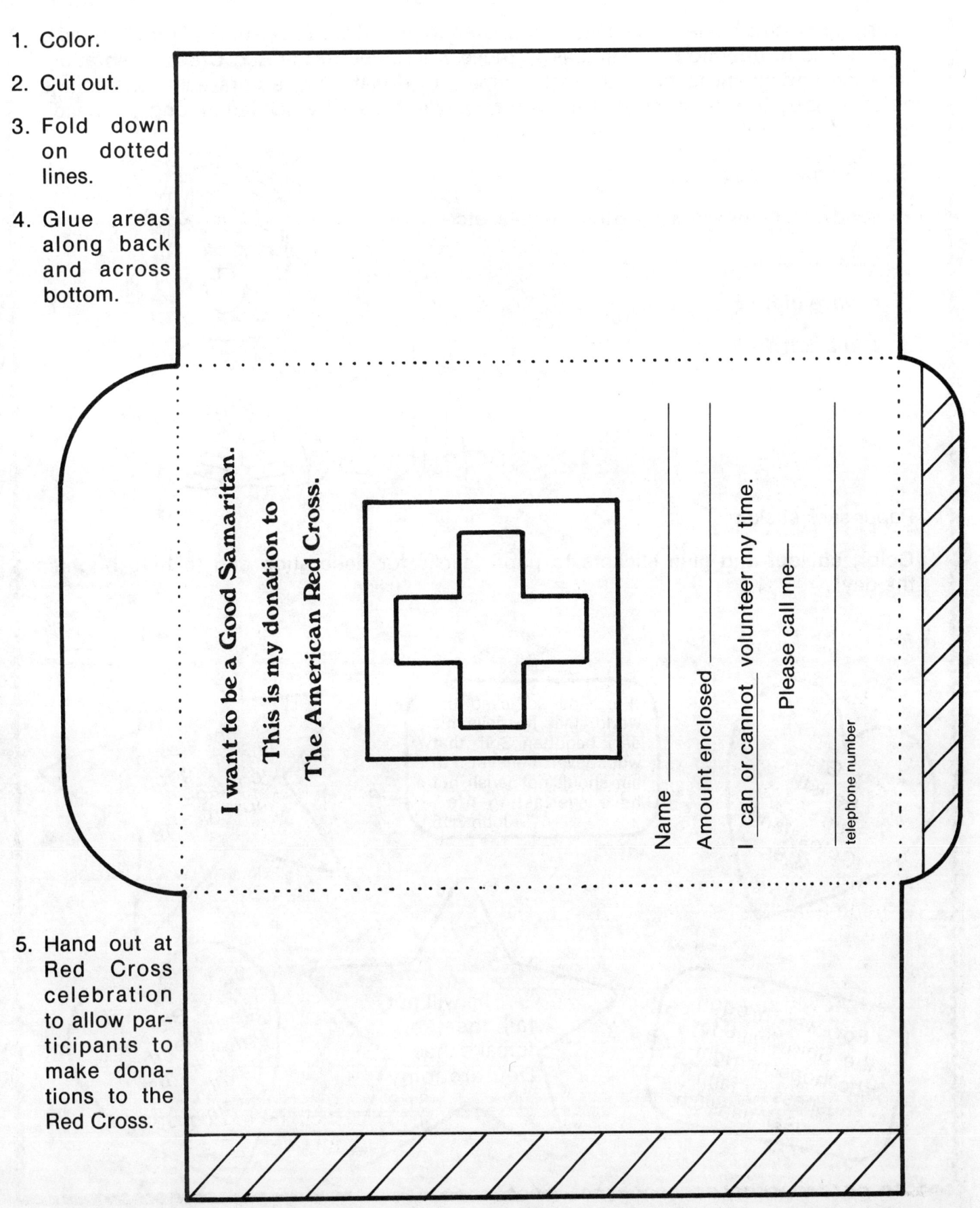

1. Color.
2. Cut out.
3. Fold down on dotted lines.
4. Glue areas along back and across bottom.

5. Hand out at Red Cross celebration to allow participants to make donations to the Red Cross.

I want to be a Good Samaritan.
This is my donation to
The American Red Cross.

Name
Amount enclosed
I can or cannot volunteer my time.
Please call me
telephone number

Shining Star Publications, Copyright © 1990, A division of Good Apple, Inc.

SS1820

"SACK SUPPER" FOR THE HOMELESS

Prearrange with a homeless shelter in your area to provide a "sack supper" for the needy. And instead of offering refreshments to those who come to the Red Cross celebration, ask each participant to bring a "sack supper" to donate. Make sure each one brings the same food in each sack so that each meal will be evenly divided among the needy people at the shelter.

"Sack Supper" suggestion:

  sandwich complete with lettuce, pickle, etc.

  a bag of chips

  a piece of fruit

  and a soft drink

Paper sack stickers:

Color, cut out and glue stickers to paper sacks for decoration and to help brighten the day!

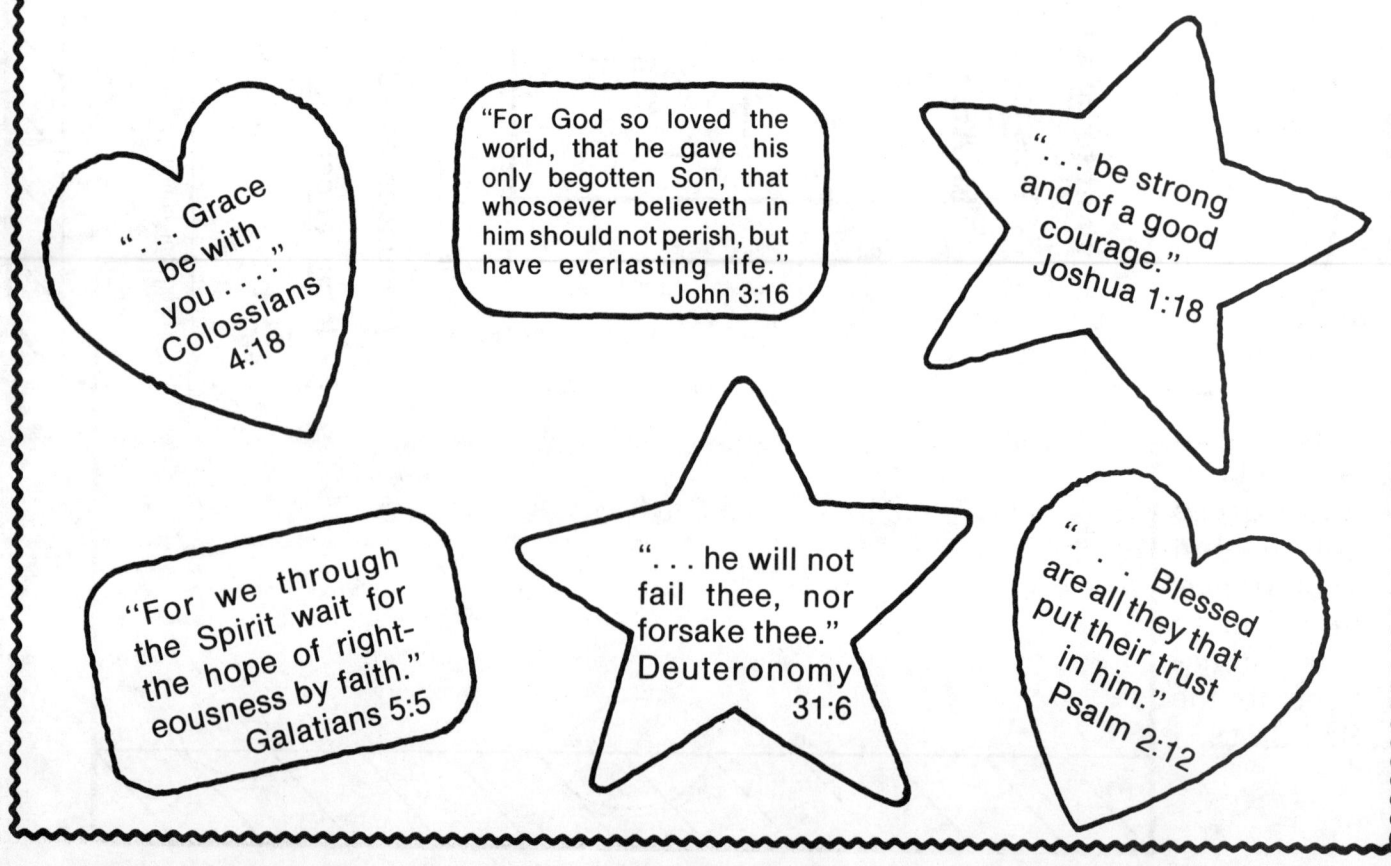

"... Grace be with you...." Colossians 4:18

"For God so loved the world, that he gave his only begotten Son, that whosoever believeth in him should not perish, but have everlasting life." John 3:16

"... be strong and of a good courage." Joshua 1:18

"For we through the Spirit wait for the hope of righteousness by faith." Galatians 5:5

"... he will not fail thee, nor forsake thee." Deuteronomy 31:6

"... Blessed are all they that put their trust in him." Psalm 2:12

Shining Star Publications, Copyright © 1990, A division of Good Apple, Inc.

SS1820

FIRST DAY OF SCHOOL CELEBRATION
DOOR POSTER: LISTEN TO THE MUSIC

(First day of school usually occurs near the end of August or the beginning of September. Check your local school calendar.)

"Serve the Lord with gladness: come before his presence with singing."

Psalm 100:2

#1 Listen to the Music
Welcome Back to School Door Decoration

1. Cover door in white paper.

2. Reproduce headset pattern provided on red paper. Cut out and tape to center of door.

3. Reproduce one musical note pattern on black paper for every student. Cut small white circles. Glue circles to rounded part of notes, and label each note with a name from the class. Tape notes to door poster. See diagram.

4. Notes may also be used as name tags if desired.

*May use as a Sunday school door poster by following the same instructions and by changing the title to:
Listen to the Music
Sing
Jesus Loves Me

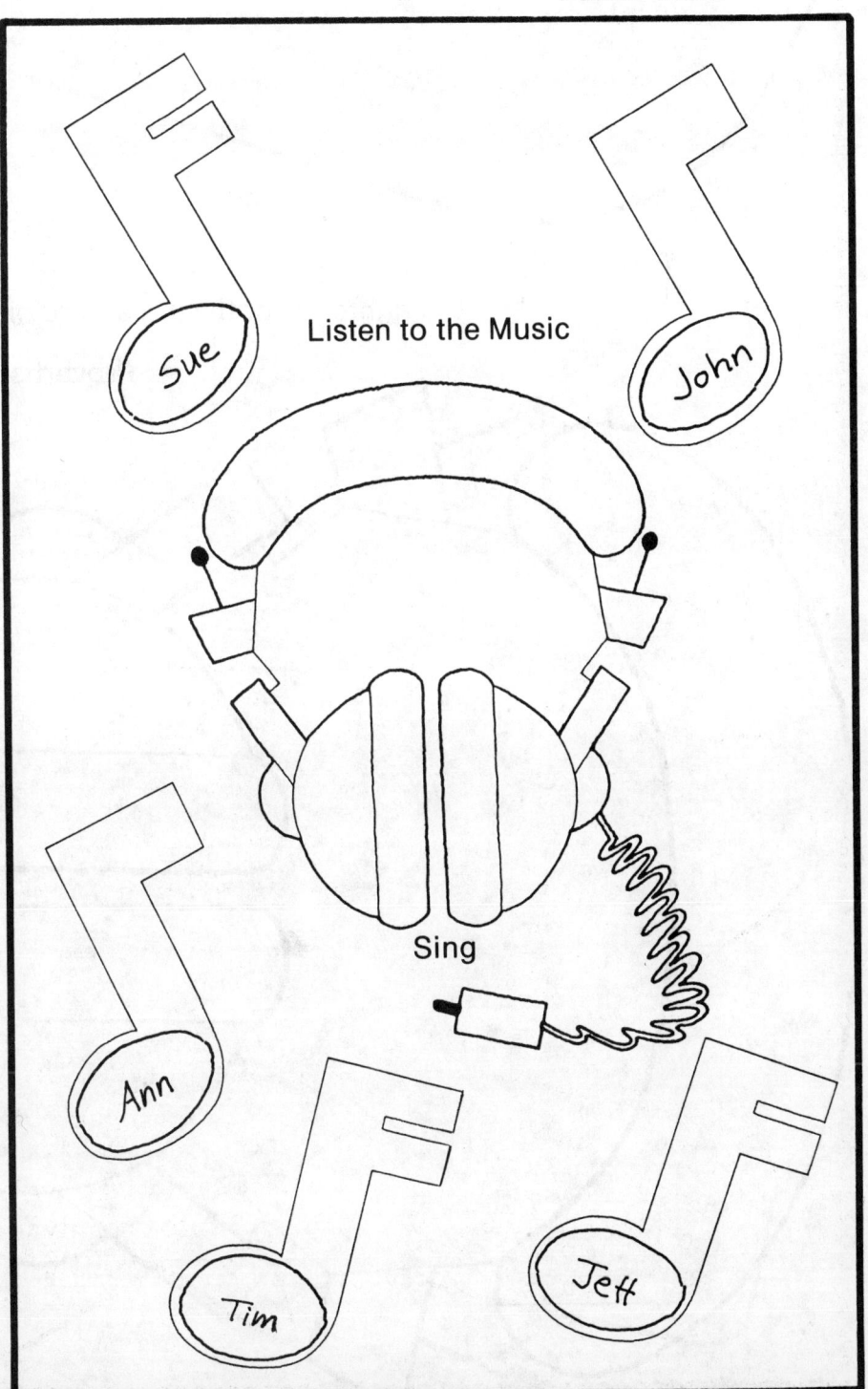

DOOR POSTER
LISTEN TO THE MUSIC

"... the righteous doth sing and rejoice."

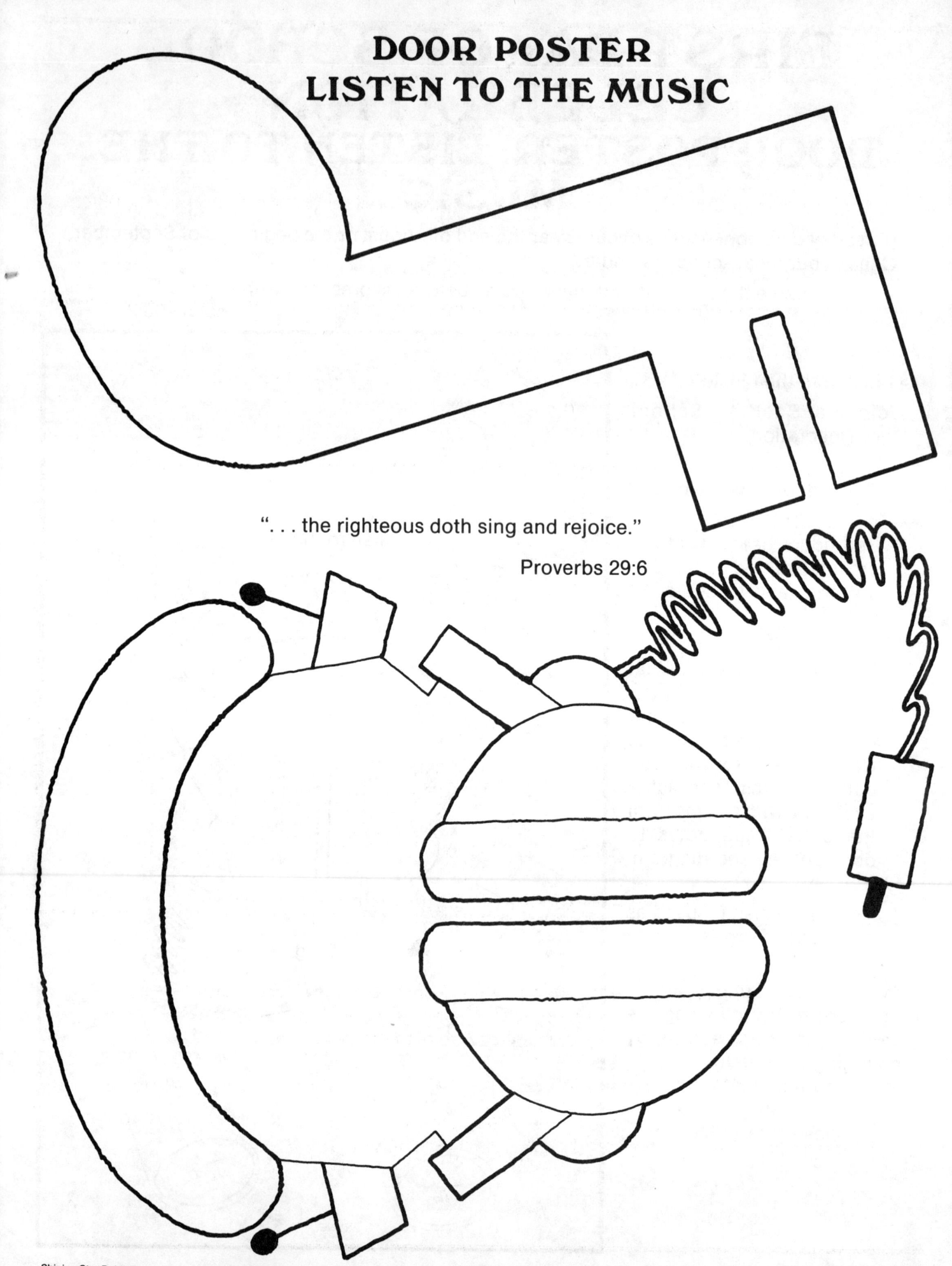

Proverbs 29:6

BULLETIN BOARD: PLAY THE NOTES THAT COUNT!

1. Cover bulletin board areas with white paper.

2. Enlarge and reproduce the cassette player pattern on red paper. Outline with black marker. Cut out and staple to bulletin board. See diagram.

3. Enlarge and reproduce note patterns on black paper.

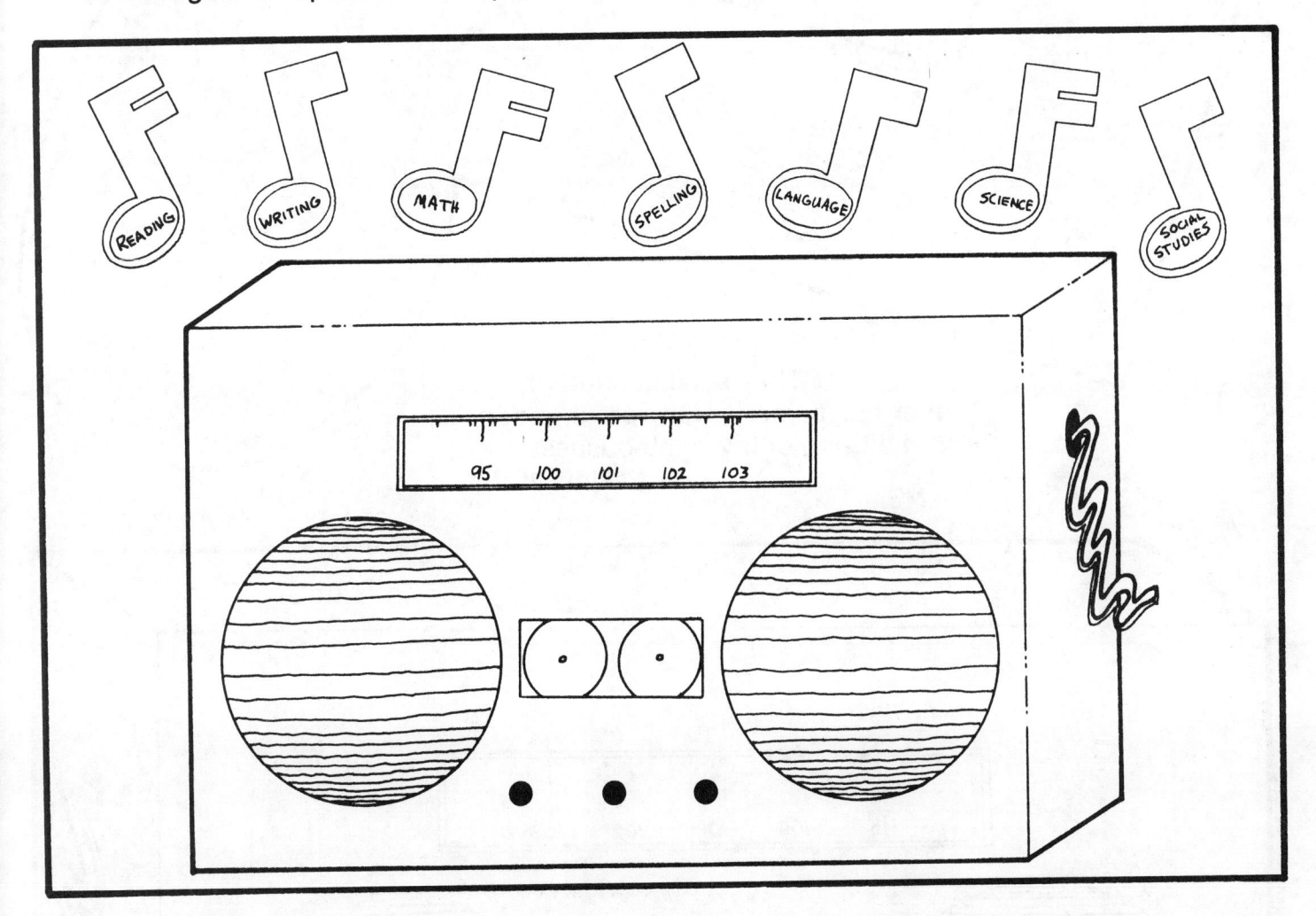

Glue small white circles to round parts of notes. Use black marker to write the names of school subjects inside each circle. Staple to bulletin board above cassette player.

4. Use black marker for bulletin board lettering.

*May use as a Sunday school bulletin board by changing the musical notes to read the titles of favorite hymns instead of study subjects in public school.

BULLETIN BOARD
PLAY THE NOTES THAT COUNT

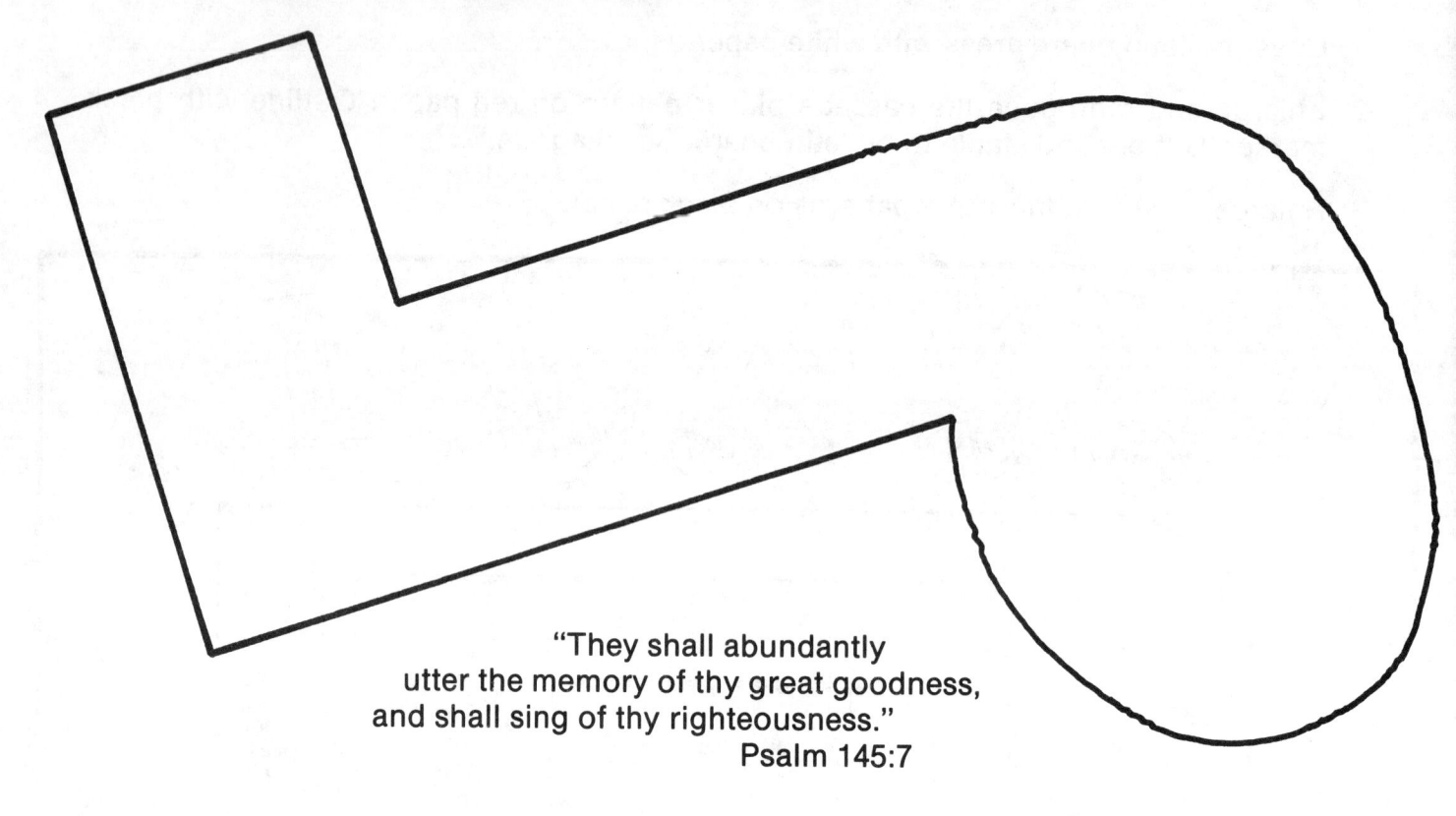

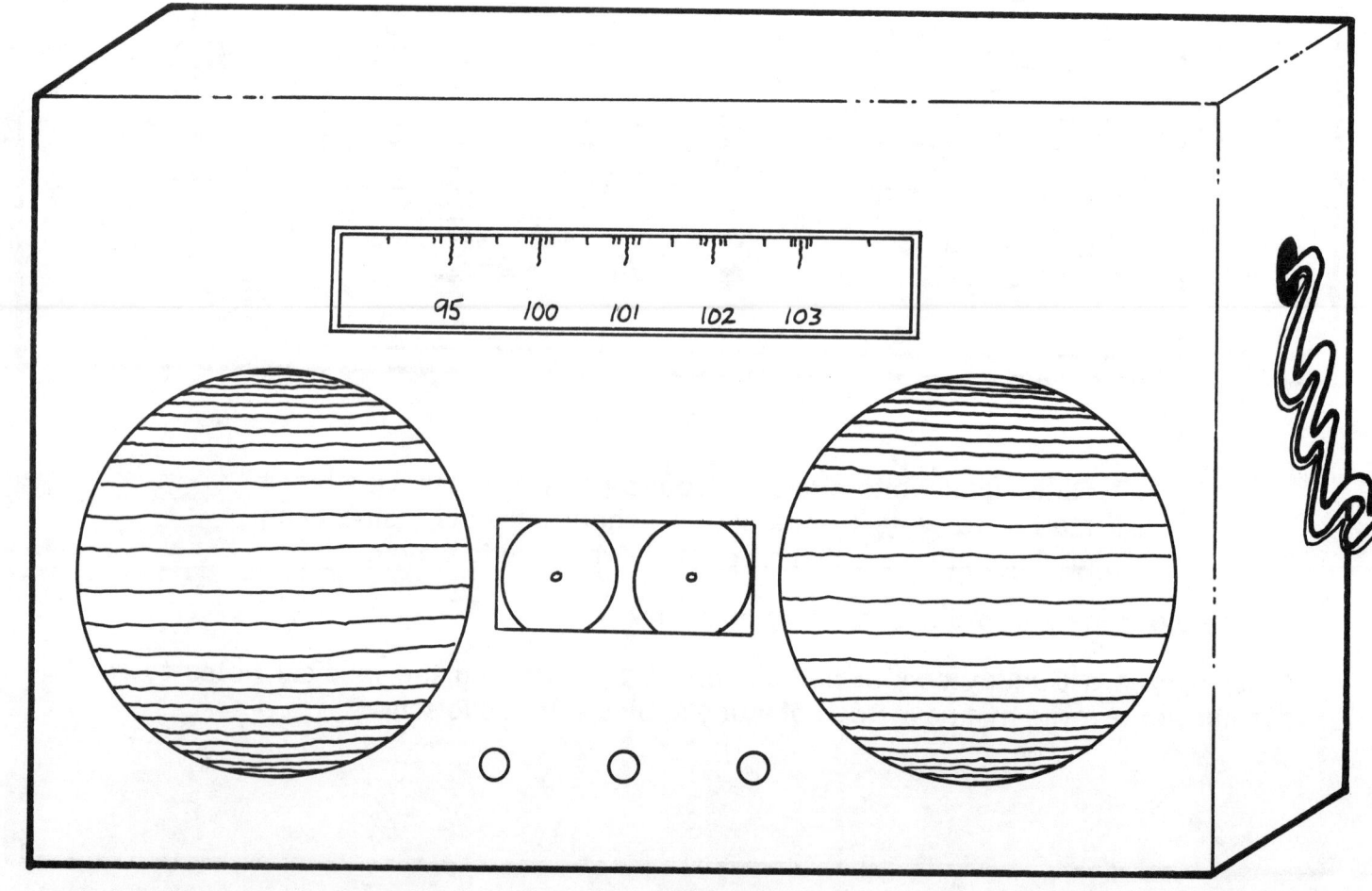

"They shall abundantly utter the memory of thy great goodness, and shall sing of thy righteousness."
Psalm 145:7

DOOR POSTER
SHOOT FOR THE STARS

#2 Shoot for the Stars

Door Decoration

"... I am the root and the offspring of David, and the bright and morning star."
Revelation 22:16

1. Cover the door with black paper.

2. Enlarge and reproduce the rocket pattern on gray paper. Cut out and tape to door. See diagram.

3. Enlarge and reproduce the star pattern on bright yellow paper. Make one for every student and use a black marker to write in a name on each star. Tape to door.

4. Use black marker for lettering.

5. Stars may also be used for name tags.

*May use as a Sunday school door poster by adding a yellow cross. See diagram below. Also use black marker to write: OUR STARS SHINE FOR CHRIST

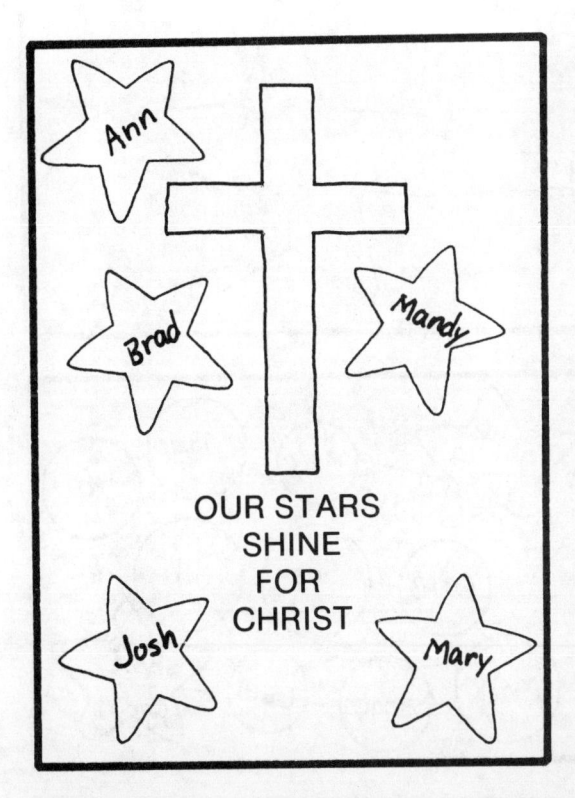

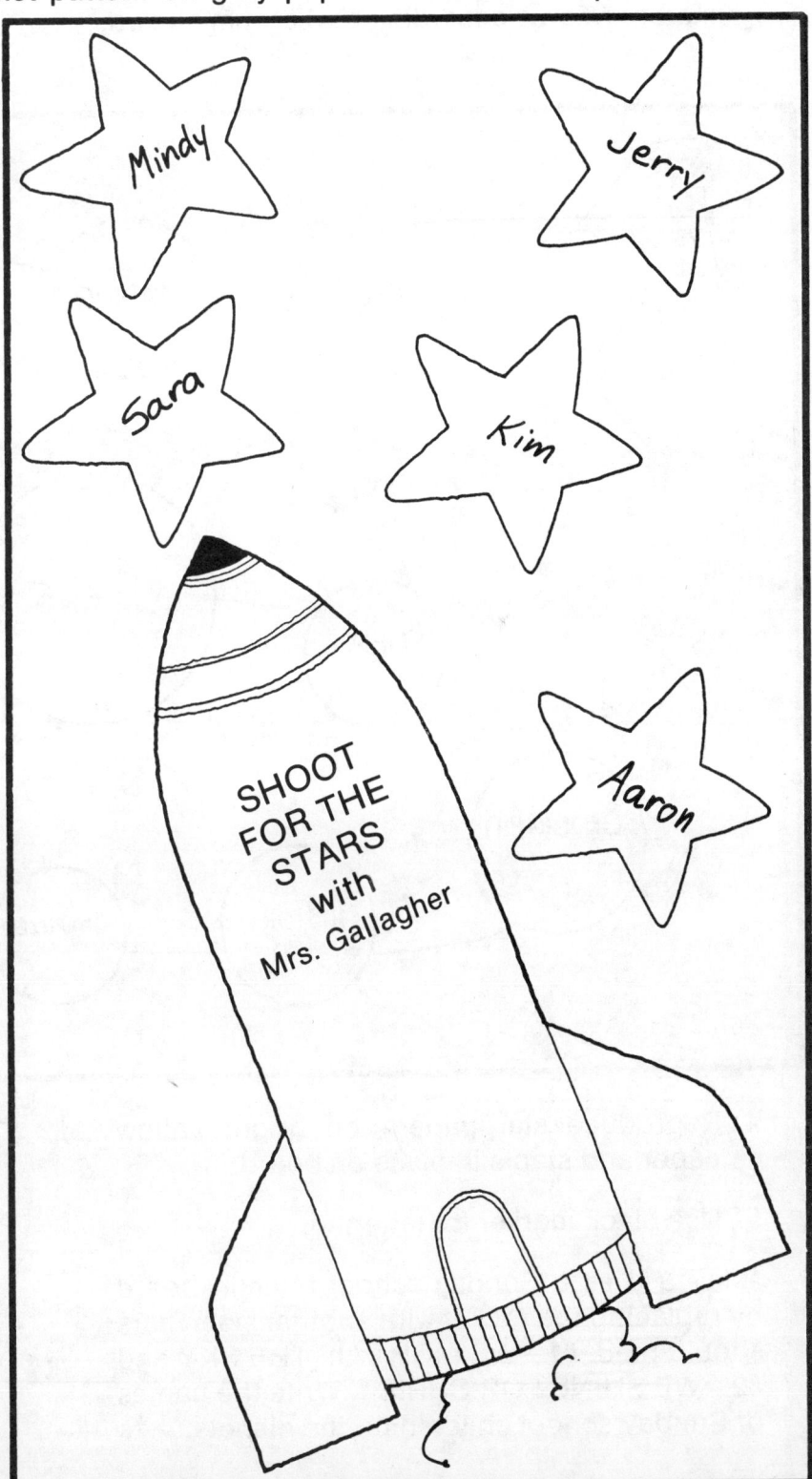

OUR STARS SHINE FOR CHRIST

SHOOT FOR THE STARS with Mrs. Gallagher

Shining Star Publications, Copyright © 1990, A division of Good Apple, Inc.

SS1820

BULLETIN BOARD
TOUR THE GALAXY

1. Cover bulletin board area with black paper.

2. Enlarge and reproduce the rocket pattern on gray paper. Cut out and staple to board.

3. Reproduce planet patterns on a mixture of brightly colored paper. Cut out and staple to board area according to diagram shown.

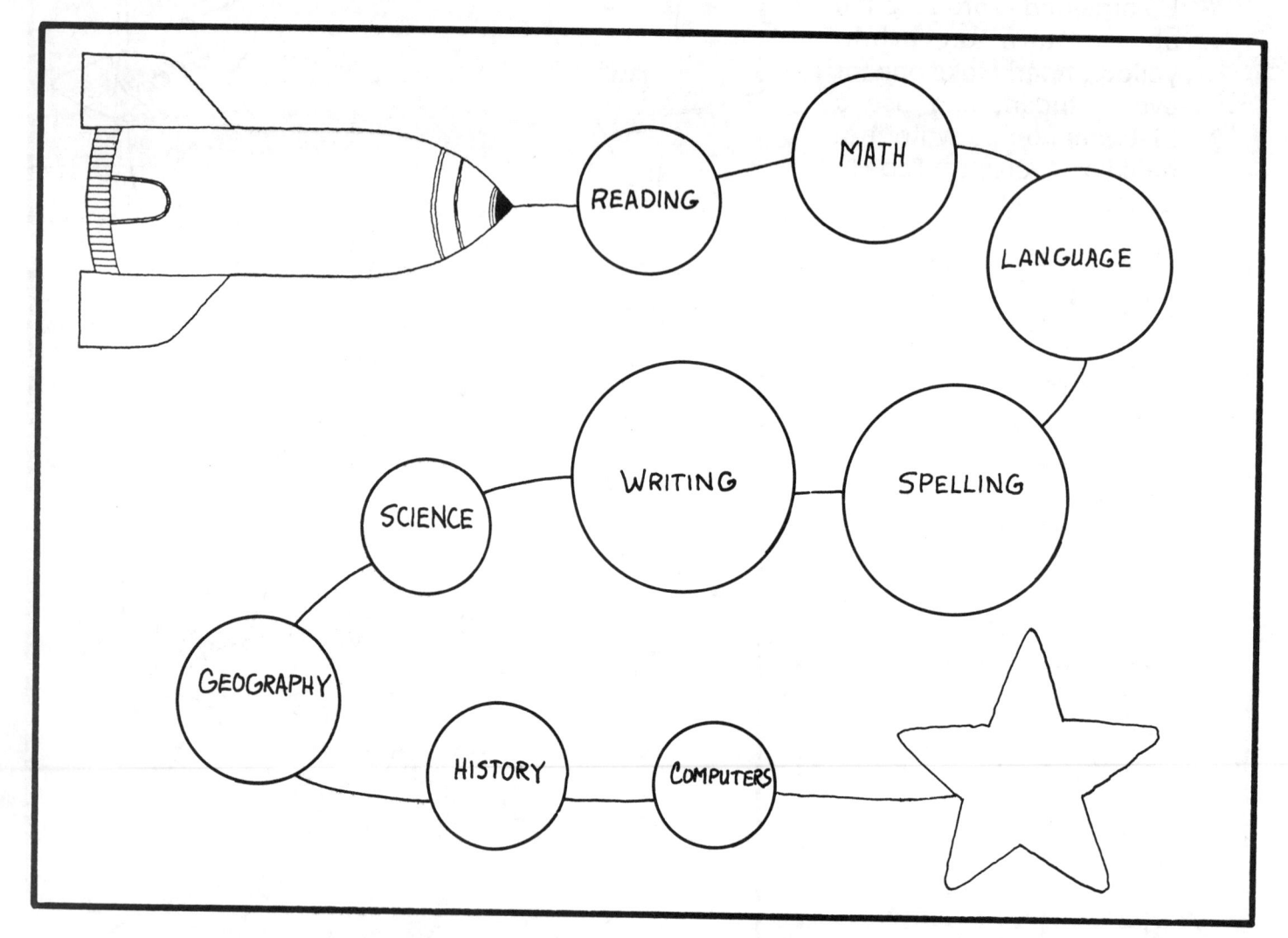

4. Reproduce star pattern on bright yellow paper and staple in place on board.

5. Use black marker for lettering.

*May use as a Sunday school bulletin board by replacing the rocket with another star. Stars should read: #1—WE LIGHT UP THE SKY and #2—WE SHINE FOR CHRIST. Write the names of Sunday school children on the planets.

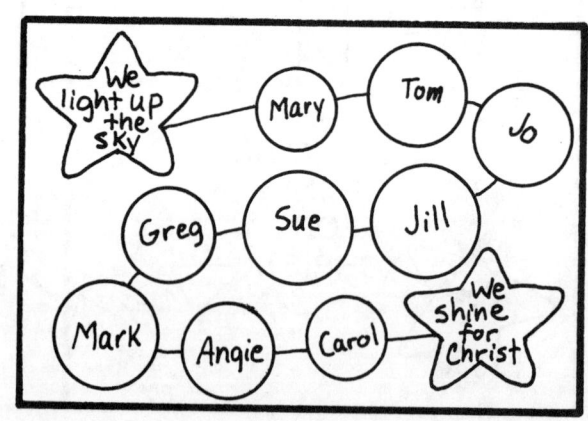

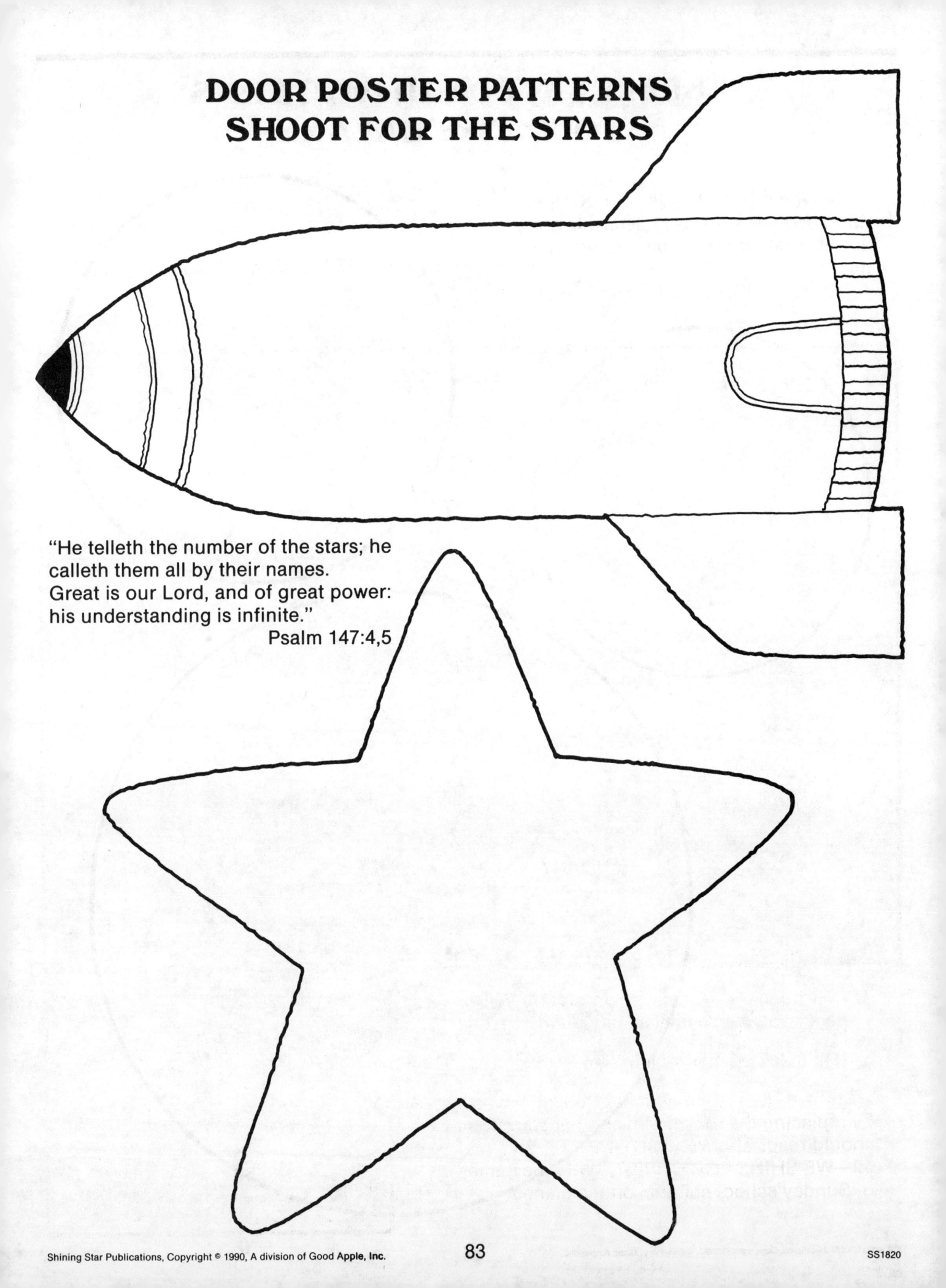

DOOR POSTER PATTERNS
SHOOT FOR THE STARS

"He telleth the number of the stars; he calleth them all by their names. Great is our Lord, and of great power: his understanding is infinite."

Psalm 147:4,5

BULLETIN BOARD PATTERNS
TOUR THE GALAXY

". . . Where is he that is born King of the Jews? for we have seen his star in the east, and are come to worship him."

Matthew 2:2

FIRST DAY OF SCHOOL CELEBRATION SNACKS

"Study to show thyself approved unto God, . . ."
II Timothy 2:15

SUGAR COOKIES

Cream: 2/3 cup shortening
3/4 cup sugar

Beat in: 1 egg
2 teaspoons vanilla
3 to 4 teaspoons of milk

Sift together: 2 cups flour
1 1/2 teaspoons baking powder

Blend creamed mixture and dry ingredients together.

Chill dough 1 to 2 hours.
Roll out on floured surface.
Cut into shapes.

Bake: 375 degrees for 5 to 10 minutes.

Use the following patterns to cut out "after-school cookies."

1. Reproduce the patterns on a heavy cardboard.
2. Cut out along the dark line.
3. Place the pattern on the rolled-out dough. Use a knife to carefully cut along the pattern.
4. Use decorative icing tubes and hard candies to decorate the cookies.

SCHOOL SNACK

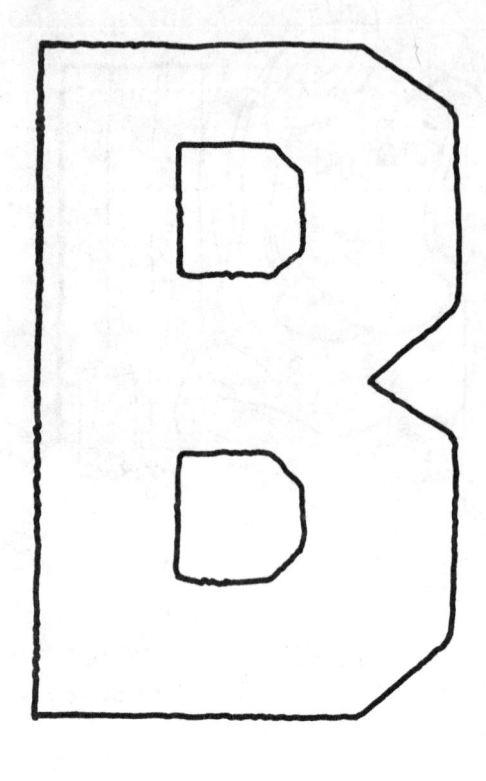

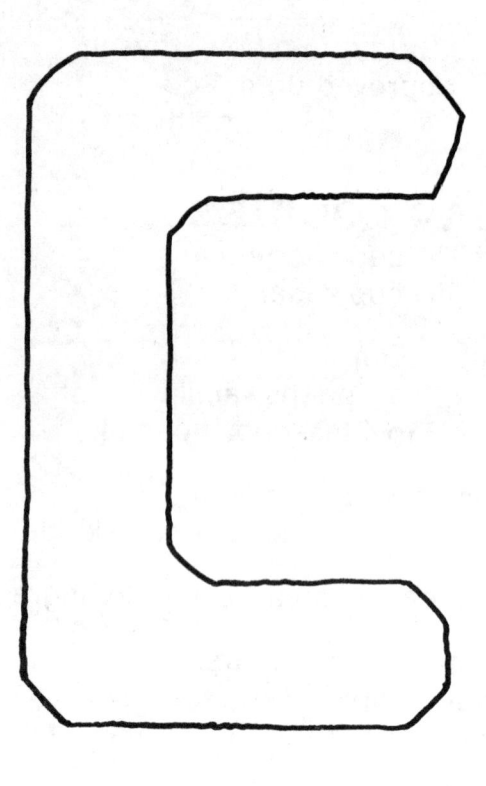

B C

2 6

GRANDPARENTS' DAY

(Celebrated in September.)

Celebrate Grandparents' Day by compiling a memory gift book for each living grandparent. Research and interview your grandparent to complete the information on the following 10 pages. Color, cut out the pages, and staple along the left-hand edge to make the book. Then, present the book to your grandparent as a celebration of his/her life.

A MEMORY GIFT BOOK

For My Grandparent

_____
Name

Compiled by _____
               Name

Age _____ Date _____

And Given in Love

Shining Star Publications, Copyright © 1990, A division of Good Apple, Inc. 87 SS1820

A MEMORY GIFT BOOK

Page 1: Birth and infant information includes date of birth, weight at birth, hair color and eye color, favorite toy, thumb sucker (?), and baby picture, if available.

"Likewise, ye younger, submit yourselves unto the elder. Yea, all of you be subject one to another, and be clothed with humility: . . ."

I Peter 5.5

My grandparent was born
_____
date

in _____, _____.
  city   state

He/She weighed _____ pounds when he/she was born.

He/She was born with _____
                      color

hair and _____ eyes.
          color

His/Her favorite baby toy was
_____.

He/She did or did not suck his/her
        circle one

thumb.

Shining Star Publications, Copyright © 1990, A division of Good Apple, Inc.

SS1820

MEMORY GIFT BOOK

Page 2: Family information includes names of great-grandparents, dates of births, places of births, and an interesting fact about each one.

My grandparent's parents are my great-grandparents.

My great-grandparents' names are:

_____
Great-grandmother

_____
Great-grandfather

My great-grandmother was born _____
                                                     date

in the state/country of _____.
                                      location

My great-grandfather was born _____
                                                     date

in the state/country of _____.
                                      location

One interesting fact about my great-grandmother was
_____.

One interesting fact about my great-grandfather was
_____.

Shining Star Publications, Copyright © 1990, A division of Good Apple, Inc.   SS1820

MEMORY GIFT BOOK

Page 3: Housing information includes location of first house, information on the strangest house and why it was the strangest, information on the favorite house and why it was the favorite.

"... the house of the righteous shall stand."
Proverbs 12:7

My grandparent has lived in _____
number

houses since he/she was born.

The first house was in

_____.

The strangest house was in _____. It was strange because _____
_____.

His/Her favorite house was in _____.
It was the favorite because
_____
_____
_____

MEMORY GIFT BOOK

Page 4: Information on grandparent's brothers and sisters includes a list of their names as well as a favorite memory about one brother or sister.

My grandparent's brothers and sisters are my great-aunts and uncles.

He/She has _____ sisters and _____ brothers.
               number   number

My great-aunts are
_____
_____
_____

My great-uncles are
_____
_____
_____

The best memory my grandparent has about a brother or sister is
_____
_____
_____

MEMORY GIFT BOOK

Page 5: Entertainment information includes parties, church socials, sleep overs, dances, movies, and others.

Back in the "good old days" my grandparent had fun growing up! His/Her favorite memories of entertainment are

PARTIES

CHURCH SOCIALS

SLEEP OVERS

MOVIES

DANCES

OTHERS

MEMORY GIFT BOOK

Page 6: Travel information includes number of miles traveled, longest trip, most exciting trip and modes of travel taken.

My grandparent must have traveled at least _____
number

miles throughout his/her life.

His/Her longest trip was to _____
location

in _____
date

The most exciting trip was to

_____
location

in _____.
date

Check the following:

My grandparent has traveled by

automobile ☐
train ☐
bus ☐
airplane ☐
wagon ☐
rocket ☐
boat ☐
motorcycle ☐
other _____

The trip was exciting because _____
_____
_____
_____

Other trips my grandparent would like to take are
_____
_____
_____

93

Shining Star Publications, Copyright © 1990, A division of Good Apple, Inc.   SS1820

MEMORY GIFT BOOK

Page 7: Education includes high school graduation, school colors, school mascot, best friends, favorite high school memory, college information, and self-taught skills.

My grandparent's education consists of the following degrees _____

He/She went to high school in _____
_{city}

and graduated in _____.
_{date}

School colors were _____.

Best friends in high school were _____, _____, _____.

Favorite high school memory was _____
_____

He/She graduated from college (check one) yes ☐ no ☐

Date graduated _____.

Name of college _____

College colors _____

College mascot _____

Best friends in college _____

Favorite college memory _____
_____.

Self-taught areas include
_____
_____
_____

MEMORY GIFT BOOK

Page 8: Job information includes number of jobs, first job, most memorable job, way of making a living, and what he/she would change if they had had the opportunity.

"O Lord, how manifold are thy works! in wisdom hast thou made them all: the earth is full of thy riches."
Psalm 104:24

My grandparent has had a total of _____ jobs during his/her lifetime.

His/Her very first job was for _____.

His/Her duties were to _____.

The job began _____ and ended _____.
              date   date

My grandparent's most memorable job was for _____.

It was memorable because _____
_____.

My grandparent made most of his living by _____. If he/she could do it over again, he/she would have become a _____.

MEMORY GIFT BOOK

Page 9: Christian information includes dates for baptism, joining the church, Christian advice, and why grandchild is proud of grandparents.

"And I say also unto thee, That thou art Peter, and upon this rock I will build my church; . . ."

Matthew 16:18

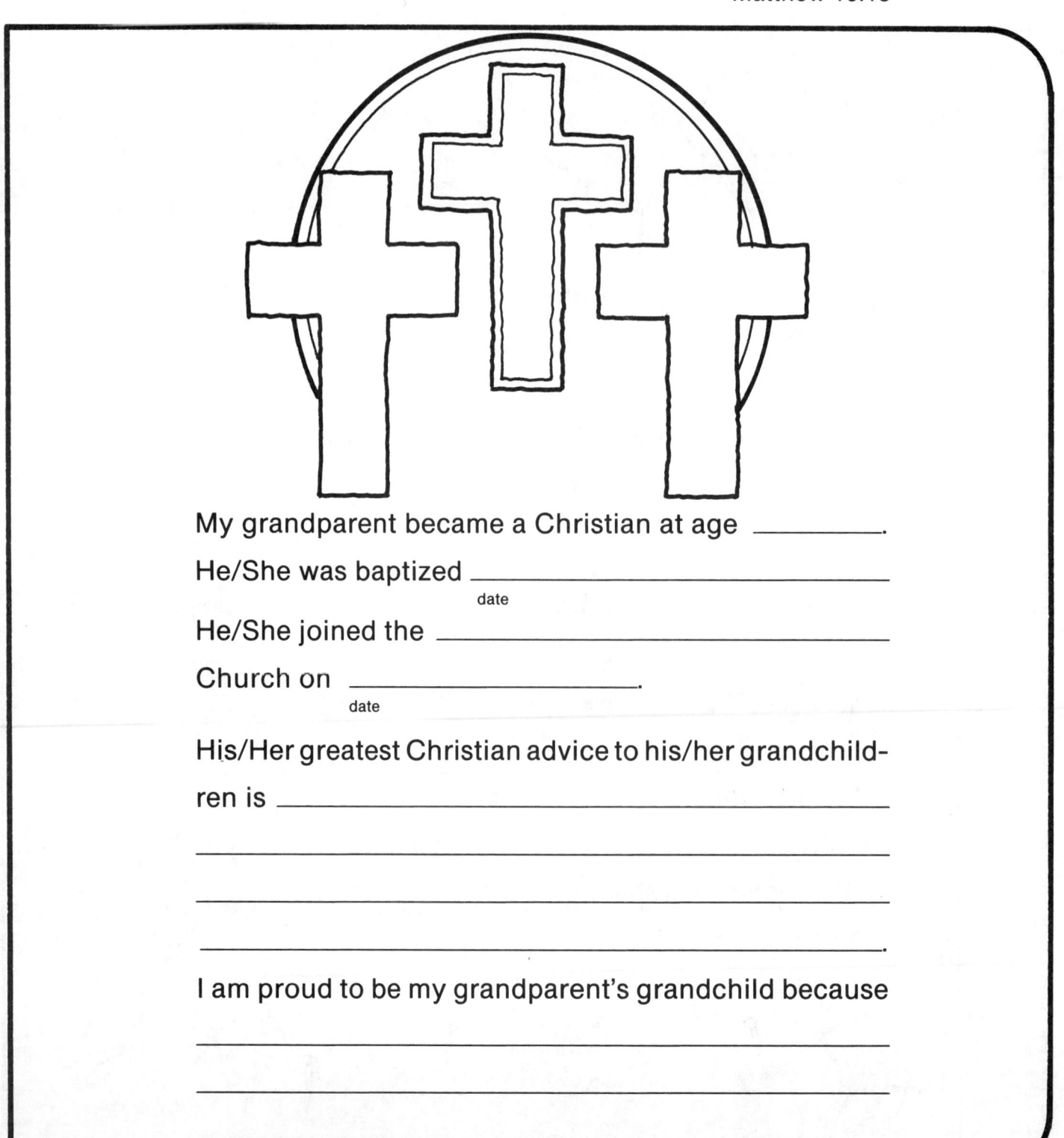

My grandparent became a Christian at age _____.

He/She was baptized _____
date

He/She joined the _____

Church on _____.
date

His/Her greatest Christian advice to his/her grandchildren is _____

_____

_____

_____.

I am proud to be my grandparent's grandchild because

_____

_____

_____